CITY LIFE-CYCLES AND AMERICAN URBAN POLICY

STUDIES IN URBAN ECONOMICS

Under the Editorship of

Edwin S. Mills
Princeton University

CITY LIFE-CYCLES AND AMERICAN URBAN POLICY

R. D. NORTON

Department of Economics
Mount Holyoke College
South Hadley, Massachusetts

ACADEMIC PRESS

New York   San Francisco   London

A Subsidiary of Harcourt Brace Jovanovich, Publishers

ACADEMIC PRESS, INC.
111 Fifth Avenue, New York, New York 10003

United Kingdom Edition published by
ACADEMIC PRESS, INC. (LONDON) LTD.
24/28 Oval Road, London NW1 7DX

Library of Congress Cataloging in Publication Data

Norton, R   D
    City life-cycles and American urban policy.

    (Studies in urban economics)
    Includes bibliographical references and index.
    1. Cities and towns--United States--Growth--Case
studies. 2. Industries, Location of--United States
--Case studies. 3. Urban policy--United States--
History. 4. Urban economics. 5. Federal aid to
community development--United States. I. Title.
II. Series.
HT123.N66   301.36'0973   79-51704
ISBN 0-12-521850-8

PRINTED IN THE UNITED STATES OF AMERICA

79 80 81 82   9 8 7 6 5 4 3 2 1

TO JOHN AND ERMA NORTON

CONTENTS

PREFACE

This book is an interdisciplinary study of differential urban development in the United States since 1945. Its purpose is to place urban policy choices in historical perspective. To that end, it asks what guidelines might shape a coherent federal response to the nation's key urban problem: the continuing concentration of the minority poor in declining older cities.

The continuing concentration of minority poverty stands in sharp contrast to the accelerating *decentralization* of industrial production, and of economic activity generally. The nineteenth-century urban–industrial transformation created both a centralized industrial city and a core industrial region, the Manufacturing Belt of the Northeast and Upper Midwest. Over the past century, this spatially polarized industrial structure has been hit by successive waves of decentralization, initially within the metropolis, then (after 1945) from the core to younger areas in the South and West and abroad, and now, it seems, from urban to rural sites.

The prospect these two divergent tendencies create is one of entrenched structural unemployment in the declining industrial cities—a problem aggravated by local political institutions that restrict the spatial mobility of the urban poor. On the premise that this prospect will eventually prove unacceptable, the book develops historical perspectives on two possible responses: economic rejuvenation of the older city, and the dispersal of the urban poor to areas offering superior job opportunities. The central issue is thus whether redevelopment or dispersal constitutes a more realistic goal for a national urban growth policy. The argument can be summarized briefly here.

Chapters 1 and 2 identify the issues and establish a framework within which relevant quantitative measurements can be interpreted. Choices concerning the two contrasting urban strategies will depend in part on perceptions of causal mechanisms. Accordingly, Chapters 3–7 develop and report systematic empirical tests, which typically take the form of regression equations.

Chapter 3 traces city population changes to two proximate causes: annexation and urban growth. A statistical model relating city growth rates to these two variables accounts for some 90% of the variation among the 30 largest cities for the 1950–1970 period, the period when growth contrasts between young and old cities were most sharply defined.

At this surface level, the explanation for such growth contrasts is clear. Young cities have benefited both from rapid urban growth and from large-scale annexation. In the older metropolis, one finds the worst of both worlds: frozen borders and sluggish areawide growth. As a result, suburbanization has taken a harsher toll on old than on young cities. On a deeper level, however, this explanation leaves a great deal to be explained. In particular, what accounts for the behavior of the two underlying growth determinants? That is, *why have annexation and urban growth varied so decisively with the timing of urban development?* The answers to these questions are central to the policy issue: city economic redevelopment or balanced dispersal?

Chapter 4 focuses on the reasons for annexation contrasts among the nation's largest cities. The chapter's historical survey suggests that annexation power varies in accordance with the differing social roles young and old cities have played.

The industrial city's traditional social use has been as a processing center for the immigrant and now the minority poor. As a result of the spatial conflict that role has engendered, the industrial city's borders have long since been frozen. By contrast, younger metropolitan areas have largely escaped this sort of spatial polarization by class and race. And annexation has remained a possibility for most young cities.

Chapters 5 and 6 deal with the second city-growth determinant, the urban growth rate. There we come to the key empirical issue for purposes of assessing a redevelopment strategy's realism. If a jobs-to-people strategy is to be pursued, its effectiveness will depend on the stabilization of the old city's declining job base. The question is, can public policy permanently reverse the industrial city's long-term job losses? The theme of the two chapters is that such job losses emanate from basic realignments within the industrial system. A result established in Chapter 5 is that a city's job performance since World War II can be traced ultimately to the performance of its SMSA's manufacturing sector. From this standpoint, the key issue is, can the older SMSA's industrial competitiveness be restored through governmental intervention?

The message of Chapter 6 is that such intervention would have to be truly massive to have much impact on the older area's industrial position. The basis for this conclusion lies in the gradual but unmistakable *dispersion of innovative capacity* from the nation's traditional seedbed, the Manufacturing Belt. The belt's older metropolitan areas are no longer able to rely on the seedbed role to counter their losses of standardized, mature industries. As a result, they have become highly vulnerable to the dispersion of manufacturing—a tendency that reached floodtide proportions during the late 1960s and early 1970s.

Thus the dilemma for policy planning: On the one hand, the resource costs of an effective redevelopment strategy (jobs to people) would be high by any standard. Yet the alternative, the people-to-jobs approach, faces enormous political obstacles, at least for now.

And there is a further consideration—one that many discussions, in fact, treat as the primary issue. Local spending and taxes range higher in old than in young cities. Such differentials enhance the competitive positions of the young cities. On this count, a rejuvenation strategy may require provisions for differential fiscal relief. But what precisely should be done depends in part on the reasons spending ranges higher in the old cities.

Chapter 7 offers an institutional explanation for fiscal differentials among large cities. The older area's heritage of city–suburban conflict shows up today in (*a*) long-frozen city boundaries and (*b*) a tradition, one going back to the boss-run political machines, of municipal responsibility for the urban poor. On both counts, most young cities differ decisively.

A statistical model finds close associations between such local institutional variables and city spending and tax levels. In other words, the old city's high spending and taxes—barriers to its economic redevelopment—are predictable consequences of its distinctive fiscal institutions. Local fiscal endowments thus reinforce the competitive advantages young cities enjoy.

Chapter 8 addresses the issue of federal fiscal assistance to declining cities. A rough taxonomy like the one used in this book can help bring out broad developmental contrasts in city economic or fiscal positions. But for purposes of designing a compensatory aid plan, one geared to hundreds or even thousands of recipient localities, the only workable approach to measuring city differences is by way of a weighted distribution formula. As the chapter shows, the formula for the distribution of Community Development Block Grants provides a useful case study in the design of a compensatory aid scheme. On the other hand, the ill-fated 1978 attempt to extend countercyclical fiscal relief shows how a badly designed formula can backfire politically. From either standpoint, quantifying an index of urban differences emerges as the key technical issue for designing an efficient federal distribution formula.

But beyond the question of technical approaches, there remains the more fundamental issue. Will the incipient urban revival (as paced by gentrification and downtown redevelopment) improve the long-term outlook for the minority poor? The answer suggested in Chapter 9 is no. Indeed, the book's message is that a permanent improvement in the position of the urban underclass must be geared to the manufacturing sector—and hence to a dispersal strategy.

ACKNOWLEDGMENTS

I am profoundly indebted to Edwin S. Mills, without whose steadfast support this book would not have been written. Both Professor Mills and Michael N. Danielson have offered an ideal blend of encouragement and rigorous guidance. I have benefited substantially from the ideas, and in some instances the advice, of Robert Averitt, William Branson, Paula England, Robert Gilpin, David Gordon, William John Hanna, Thomas Vietorisz, and Julian Wolpert. In addition, I am uniquely obliged to Elsie M. Watters, who gave me my start.

Mark Flolid, Beth Yarbrough, and Robert Yarbrough, true Texans all, have provided most generous help with computations.

CITY LIFE-CYCLES AND
AMERICAN URBAN POLICY

1

CITIES IN EVOLUTION

Many American cities have lost people and jobs more or less steadily for the past three decades. By 1975, for example, such older cities as St. Louis, Pittsburgh, Buffalo, and Cleveland had lost 30% or more of their 1950 populations. In the same period, and as if to replace them, younger cities like San Diego, Phoenix, and Houston more than doubled in size (Table 1-1).

During the mid-1970s, urban policy discussion therefore came to focus on the declining older cities. "The declining cities," it was said, "are going through a process of urban natural selection."[1] More pointedly, "The Northern-tier urban centers are declining because they are functionally obsolete."[2] In a harsh echo of Jane Jacobs' 1961 book, an essay "On the Death of Cities" portrayed the abandonment of entire neighborhoods in numerous older cities.[3]

1. William Gorham and Nathan Glazer, *The Urban Predicament* (Washington, D.C.: The Urban Institute, 1976), p. 28.
2. Michael F. Borgos, in a letter to *Business Week,* 20 February 1978.
3. William C. Baer, "On the Death of Cities," *The Public Interest,* 45 (Fall 1976), p. 8; Jane Jacobs, *The Death and Life of Great American Cities* (New York: Random House, 1961).

TABLE 1-1
Population Changes in the 30 Largest Cities, 1950-1975[a]

City, by size of population loss or gain	Percentage change in city population, 1950-1975	Estimated population in 1975 (thousands)
St. Louis	− 39	525
Pittsburgh	− 32	459
Cleveland	− 30	639
Buffalo	− 30	407
Detroit	− 28	1335
Boston	− 21	637
Cincinnati	− 18	413
Chicago	− 14	3099
San Francisco	− 14	665
Philadelphia	− 12	1816
Washington	− 11	712
Baltimore	− 10	852
New York	− 5	7482
New Orleans	− 2	560
Kansas City	+ 3	473
Seattle	+ 4	487
Milwaukee	+ 4	666
Denver	+ 17	485
Atlanta	+ 32	436
Los Angeles	+ 38	2727
Columbus	+ 42	536
Memphis	+ 67	661
Indianapolis	+ 67	715
Dallas	+ 87	813
San Antonio	+ 89	773
Houston	+123	1327
San Diego	+131	774
Nashville	+143	423
Jacksonville	+162	535
Phoenix	+522	665

Source: U.S. Bureau of the Census, *U.S. Census of Population: 1970, Number of Inhabitants [Final Report PC(1)-A1]*, **United States Summary;** and **Current Population Reports,** Series P-25, Nos. 649-698, 1977.

[a] These are the 30 largest cities as of the 1970 Census, and as reported in U.S. Bureau of the Census, *U.S. Census of Population: 1970, Number of Inhabitants [Final Report PC(1)-A1]*, *United States Summary,* Table 28.

As the national economy moved out of the 1975 recession, perceptions changed accordingly, but accounts of urban conditions continued to rely on biological imagery. By 1979, for example, media reports were describing an urban renaissance: a rebirth of downtown areas, and of nearby neighborhoods.[4] Now the focus shifted to the ways older cities were adapting to a changing environment.

In either context, the use of biological analogies acknowledges an evolutionary dynamic that has dominated American urban development since 1945. Such a dynamic reveals itself most clearly in the divergent growth trajectories of younger and older cities, metropolitan areas, and regions—divergences, that is, between spatial structures of differing "ages." In the face of these overriding processes of age-correlated growth and decline, public policy has at times seemed almost irrelevant.

This book explores the economic and political content of a particularly ambitious biological analogy, that of the city life-cycle. The idea of a systematic cycle of urban development and decay can be traced back, via Lewis Mumford's *The Culture of Cities* (1938), to Patrick Geddes' *Cities in Evolution* (1915).[5] But only in the latter half of the 1960s did references to an American city life-cycle become widespread.[6]

In a 1966 essay, for example, James Q. Wilson comments, "Cities, like people, pass through life-cycles during which their values and functions change."[7] To set the stage for the book's larger argument, this opening chapter summarizes what others have said about just that issue: *How do a city's functions change as it ages?* The place to begin, of course, is at the beginning, with the city's economic functions.

---

4. See, for example, Blake Fleetwood, "The New Elite and an Urban Renaissance," *The New York Times Magazine*, 14 January 1979, pp. 16 *et seq.*; and "A City Revival?" in *Newsweek*, 15 January 1979, pp. 28-35.

5. Patrick Geddes, *Cities in Evolution* (New York: Oxford University Press, revised and edited edition, 1950); Lewis Mumford, *The Culture of Cities* (New York: Harcourt, Brace, 1938), pp. 283-292. See also S. A. Queen and L. F. Thomas, "The Life Cycle of American Cities," chapter 22 of *The City: The Study of Urbanism in the United States* (New York: McGraw-Hill, 1939).

6. See John R. Borchert, "American Metropolitan Evolution," *Geographical Review*, 57 (1967), pp. 301-332; Jay W. Forrester, *Urban Dynamics* (Cambridge: MIT Press, 1969); and David L. Birch, *The Economic Future of City and Suburb* (New York: Committee for Economic Development, 1970).

7. James Q. Wilson, "The War on Cities," *The Public Interest*, 3 (Spring 1966), reprinted in *The Modern City: Readings in Urban Economics*, eds. David W. Rasmussen and Charles T. Haworth (New York: Harper & Row, 1973), p. 24.

CITIES, INNOVATION, AND ECONOMIC DEVELOPMENT

American urban development has been instrumental to national economic growth—that is, to the accumulation of capital. The economic aging of cities can thus be viewed as a byproduct of the industrial system's evolution. This section offers one such appraisal. It explores the relationship between city economic positions and technological innovation—the rejuvenating force that drives the economy's development.

CREATIVE DESTRUCTION

As long ago as 1848, Marx and Engels realized that Britain's Industrial Revolution had brought a system of permanent technological transformation. As they wrote of Britain's early industrialists,

> The bourgeoisie cannot exist without constantly revolutionising the instruments of production, and thereby the relations of production, and with them the whole relations of society. . . . All fixed, fast-frozen relations . . . are swept away, all new-formed ones become antiquated before they can ossify.[8]

Hence Joseph Schumpeter, who is more commonly identified with the study of technological change, would write of the fact "long ago emphasized by . . . Marx . . . that in dealing with capitalism we are dealing with an evolutionary process [a system that] not only never is but never can be stationary."[9]

According to Schumpeter, innovation's role as the source of supranormal profit makes it the "fundamental impulse that sets and keeps the capitalist engine in motion." In a passage central to our theme, he writes that innovation sets off a

> process of industrial mutation—if I may use that biological term—that incessantly revolutionizes the economic structure *from within*, in-

---

8. Karl Marx and Frederick Engels, *Manifesto of the Communist Party* (Peking: Foreign Languages Press, 1972), pp. 34–35.

9. Joseph A. Schumpeter, *Capitalism, Socialism, and Democracy*, paperback edition (New York, Harper & Row, 1962) of 1942 original, p. 82.

cessantly destroying the old one, incessantly creating a new one. This process of Creative Destruction is the essential fact about capitalism.[10]

AMERICAN CITIES AS INDUSTRIAL ARTIFACTS

The evolutionary process of interest is thus not biological in character, but technological. In an American context, technological change means spatial upheaval, because the nation's traditional urban and regional structure derives from the highly specific technological constraints of the brief period between about 1880 and 1914. Of that period's formative role, Wilbur Thompson writes, "We did not, for the most part, build great cities in this country; manufacturing firms agglomerated in tight industrial complexes and formed labor market pools of half a million workers."[11]

Beyond the Eastern seaboard, the settlement of the United States was contemporary with its nineteenth-century economic transformation.[12] Places that prospered were thus well suited to the competition for functions within the classical industrial regime. By the same token, however, large American cities have been more vulnerable to subsequent changes in the economic environment than, say, the great European capitals. In particular, they have been vulnerable to the technological changes reshaping the location of manufacturing—the sector that sparked the whirlwind growth of today's older cities in the decades before World War I.

POLARIZED DEVELOPMENT AS A SPATIAL LEGACY

Such growth had a remarkably concentrated spatial form. The technologies of the industrial revolution encouraged highly centralized spatial structures: not only centralized cities, but also a core region. Industrialization per se was largely confined to the Northeast quadrant, the "Manufacturing Belt." In turn, and as a concomitant of

---

10. *Ibid.*, pp. 83–84.

11. Wilbur Thompson, "Economic Processes and Employment Problems in Declining Urban Areas," in *Post-Industrial America: Metropolitan Decline and Inter-Regional Job Shifts*, eds. George Sternlieb and James W. Hughes (New Brunswick: Center for Urban Policy Research, 1975), p. 189.

12. Lance E. Davis *et al.*, *American Economic Growth: An Economist's History of the United States* (New York: Harper & Row, 1972), p. 128.

industrialization, urban development varied strikingly as between this core region and the economy's geographical periphery.

On the eve of World War I, for example, the proportion of the population living in urban places ranged up to 70% in New England, the most developed part of the economy.[13] By contrast, barely 20% of the population was urban in the still preindustrial South (Figure 1-1).

MANUFACTURING: THE LINCHPIN

This, then, was the setting for the explosive decentralization of production that would mark the decades after 1945. The economic transformation left an industrial core and a less developed periphery—the one with early and extensive urban development, and the other, mainly rural. Within this setting, technological change can be understood as a succession of impulses severing one after another of the initial centralizing ties, redirecting investment not only to the suburbs, but to the South and West, and abroad.

The general decentralization of manufacturing—both within the older metropolis and away from it altogether—will be singled out later as the ultimate source of the older city's decline. While the reasoning will differ, our findings will coincide with those David Birch, arrived at in a 1970 study—that *"the older a city gets, the less its tendency to rely on manufacturing for growth."*[14]

As a first approximation, at least, this is the conclusion we have sought as to how a city's economic functions change as it ages. In the long term, the common denominator of the growing younger city has been a healthy manufacturing sector, and that of the declining older city, large and cumulative employment losses in manufacturing.

THE SOCIAL AND POLITICAL USES OF OLDER CITIES

Does the older city's continuing contraction mean that it is "functionally obsolete"? In some declining cities, of course, depopulation has been accompanied by the shift to new and more specialized

---

13. David Ward, *Cities and Immigrants: A Geography of Change in Nineteenth Century America* (New York: Oxford University Press, 1971), p. 40, using data appearing originally in Harvey S. Perloff *et al., Regions, Resources, and Economic Growth* (Baltimore: Johns Hopkins Press, 1960), pp. 172–183.

14. Birch, *The Economic Future of City and Suburb,* p. 13. (Emphasis added.)

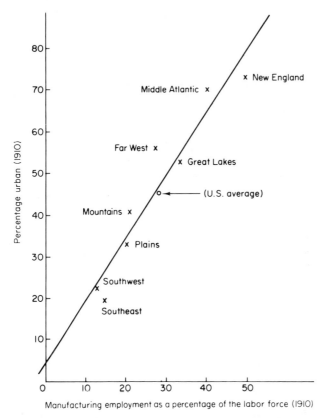

Figure 1-1. Regional urbanization in 1910, as a function of regional industrialization. Regional groupings follow Perloff **et al.,** as cited in the text. $Y = 4.76 + 1.52X$; $N = 8$, $R^2 = .92$.

economic roles, or functions. But even beyond this sort of economic adaptation, there are compelling reasons to reject such a label.

One is that the sources of city decline are in part institutional. Unlike regions or metropolitan areas, legal cities are more administrative constructs than distinct economic or spatial entities. As such, they cover varying shares of their metropolitan areas, shares that depend on the ease with which new territory can be annexed. As Table 1-2 shows, most growing cities expanded their legal land areas dramatically after 1950, and most declining ones had frozen boundaries. In this sense, whether a city grows or declines is partly an administrative outcome.

TABLE 1-2

Annexation and Population Growth in the 30 Largest Cities, 1950-1975
(Percentage Changes)

City, by relative population gain or loss	City population gain/loss	City territory gain	SMSA population gain[a]
Phoenix	+522	1499	267
Jacksonville	+162	2436	93
Nashville	+143	2208	50
San Diego	+131	225	185
Houston	+123	206	142
San Antonio	+ 89	279	80
Dallas	+ 87	176	110
Indianapolis	+ 67	580	58
Memphis	+ 67	169	50
Columbus	+ 42	338	69
Los Angeles	+ 38	3	67
Atlanta	+ 32	256	104
Denver	+ 17	70	128
Milwaukee	+ 4	90	41
Seattle	+ 4	18	67
Kansas City	+ 3	292	49
New Orleans	− 2	0	54
New York	− 5	0	5
Baltimore	− 10	0	47
Washington	− 11	0	97
Philadelphia	− 12	1	31
San Francisco	− 14	2	46
Chicago	− 14	7	35
Cincinnati	− 18	4	35
Boston	− 21	0	54
Detroit	− 28	0	40
Buffalo	− 30	5	22
Cleveland	− 30	1	29
Pittsburgh	− 32	2	5
St. Louis	− 39	0	32

Source: Column 1: Same as for Table 1-1. Column 2: U.S. Bureau of the Census, *1950 Census of Population, Vol. 1, Number of Inhabitants, United States Summary;* and *Boundary and Annexation Survey 1970-1975,* 1978. Column 3: U.S. Bureau of the Census, *Current Population Reports,* Series P-25, No. 709, September 1977; and first source listed for Column 2.

[a] 1975 SMSA territorial definitions have been used to measure 1950 as well as 1975 SMSA population.

In any case, even declining cities can retain noneconomic functions. Consider, for example, Irving Kristol's observation: "Americans have always *used* their cities, and more often than not in a casual and even brutal way."[15] Along with the older city's traditional use as an economic center, he sees a corresponding social use, as a "kind of service station":

> One service, in particular, has been of the utmost importance: the absorption and integration of rural immigrants—mainly, but not only, foreign—into American life.... The American city is an entrepot, importing people and exporting citizens to the suburban towns and smaller suburban cities.[16]

THE RESERVATION ISSUE

As this passage implies, the traditional social use of the older city has been as an upgrading center or "zone of passage" for the immigrant and (to a lesser degree) the minority poor.[17] In the past, upgrading occurred because the older city generated sufficient demand for unskilled labor that rural migrants and their children could entertain hopes of eventual access to the American mainstream. Since 1945, however, the older city's secular job losses have severely abridged its upgrading capacity—as has the changing employment mix characterizing its contracting economy.

This growing imbalance between its social and economic roles has led Norton Long to describe the older city not as an upgrading center, but as a kind of reservation for a dependent underclass.[18] Similarly, in an interview entitled "Are Big Cities Worth Saving?" George Sternlieb has answered that they are indeed, as "sandboxes" for the minority poor, places their energy and anger can be contained.[19]

---

15. Irving Kristol, "An Urban Civilization Without Cities?" *Washington Post,* 3 December 1972.

16. *Ibid.*

17. James Heilbrun, "Poverty and Public Finance in the Older Central Cities," in *Readings in Urban Economics,* eds. Matthew Edel and Jerome Rothenberg (New York: Macmillan, 1972), pp. 544–545.

18. Norton Long, "The City as Reservation," *The Public Interest,* 25 (Fall 1971) pp. 22–38.

19. George Sternlieb, "Are Big Cities Worth Saving?" *U.S. News and World Report,* 26 July 1971, pp. 42–49. See also his "The City as Sandbox," *The Public Interest,* 25 (Fall 1971).

These labels date from essays published in 1971. Despite media discussion of the urban revival of the late 1970s, there are indications that ghetto labor market conditions were actually worse at the end of the decade than at its beginning.[20] To that extent, the reservation issue has become more acute.

The declining older cities may thus retain a crucial noneconomic function. As de facto reservations for the minority poor, *they may insulate much of the population from poverty's spillover costs.* By the same token, the plight of the minority poor themselves is aggravated by their spatial concentration—and their distance from suburban, Sunbelt, and rural job growth.

DO WE WANT A PERMANENT URBAN UNDERCLASS?

How the federal government should respond to the industrial city's emerging role as a reservation is of course a political question. One possibility is to let nature take its course. Indeed, one could argue that under the "benign neglect" of the Nixon and Ford administrations, the implicit strategy was to sanction the reservation outcome. More recently, the reservation strategy has been championed by *Fortune* magazine, which declares, "It's Up to the Cities to Save Themselves."[21]

Whatever its short-run political appeal, in the long run the laissez-faire approach to the older city's decline is laced with hazards. It creates the prospect of a permanent urban underclass, quarantined by what M. N. Danielson has termed *The Politics of Exclusion*—the system of "snob zoning," building code enforcement, and real estate practices designed to keep the minority poor out of the older metropolis's more prosperous suburbs.[22]

It is this political restriction of spatial mobility that sets the declining industrial city apart from other instances of spatial decline. While spatial decline generally can be expected to trigger outmigration on the part of job seekers, the older city's decline is complicated by en-

---

20. In particular, black teenage unemployment levels were substantially higher at the end of the 1970s, edging toward 40%, than they had been early in the decade. See Alfred L. Malabre, "Through Good Times and Bad, Joblessness among Young Blacks Keeps Right On Rising," *Wall Street Journal,* 1 February 1979.

21. Gurney Breckenridge, *Fortune,* March 1977, pp. 194–206.

22. New York: Columbia University Press, 1976.

TABLE 1-3
Urban Strategies in Relation to the Uses of Older Cities

Strategy	Goal	
	Social use as "reservation"	Diminishing economic use
Reservation	Accept	Accept
Rejuvenation	Accept	Counter
Dispersal	Counter	Accept

trenched institutional barriers to the dispersal of the minority poor. Insofar as they succeed, such barriers perpetuate conditions that are likely to spark recurring urban crises—future crises of social control, like that of the 1960s, and of the early 1940s, and of the years just after World War I.

The prospect of urban violence is by no means the only reason to prefer alternatives to the laissez-faire approach. Another is the injustice of institutional arrangements and practices that compound the problems of the minority poor by isolating them in deteriorating neighborhoods far from areas of job growth. This moral concern has led Anthony Downs, for example, to propose a concerted program of action for *Opening Up the Suburbs*.[23]

A third reason concerns the sheer public expense of supporting— and, in the limit, controlling—a dependent underclass. Heretofore, such costs have fallen disproportionately to the governments of the older cities, and hence to taxpayers. As Chapter 7 shows, such costs have almost certainly accelerated the economic decline of the cities themselves, and thus aggravated the structural imbalance.

A more positive federal response to the older city's decline would attempt either to shore up the city's economic functions or to disperse the minority poor to growing areas. In this opening chapter, we have traced a fundamental urban problem, that of entrenched structural unemployment, to an imbalance in the older city's economic and social functions. Both the rejuvenation and the dispersal approaches would aim to right the balance, and so to restore the process of labor-force upgrading from the bottom up (Table 1-3).

23. New Haven: Yale University Press, 1973.

The purpose of this book is to provide historical perspectives on these two urban policy strategies: rejuvenation and dispersal. The next chapter establishes a framework within which the two can be systematically compared.

APPENDIX: POSTINDUSTRIALISM – FALSE PROMISES?

There is a quite different view of the older American city's changing economic function—one that plays down manufacturing's strategic role and emphasizes services activities. Since 1920, of course, the nation's employment structure has been marked by declining primary (land-based) employment and a relatively stable secondary (goods-producing) sector. In recent decades, the economy's secular job growth has come almost exclusively from the tertiary (services) sector—a shift prompting references to "postindustrial" society and to "The First Service Economy."[24]

In recent years, postindustrialism has also come to signify a so-called *quaternary* sector.[25] This fourth category is actually drawn from the others; it refers to the information-intensive activities of administration and control that interweave the goods and services sectors. By one account, quaternary employment has exceeded that of any other (adjusted) sector since 1960, and has recently leveled off at just under 50% of the work force.[26]

INFORMATION CITY

The view emphasizing the services and information sectors in the economy's development implies a new and perhaps rejuvenating economic function for the older city—that is, to serve a global technocratic elite (the "new cosmopolites") as an information exchange:

> For those who are tuned into the international communications circuits, cities have utility precisely because they are rich in information.... To them the city is essentially a massive communications switchboard through which human interaction takes place ... the new

24. For example, Victor Fuchs, "The First Service Economy," *The Public Interest*, 2 (Winter 1966), pp. 7–17.

25. See Jean Gottman, "Urban Centrality and the Interweaving of Quaternary Activities," *Ekistics*, 29 (1970), pp. 322–331.

26. Marc Porat, *The Information Economy*, as reported in Leonard Silk, "Study for Congress: Slower Growth Ahead," *New York Times*, 9 February 1978.

cosmopolites belong to none of the world's metropolitan areas, although they use them. They belong, rather, to the national and international communities that merely maintain information exchanges at these metropolitan junctions.[27]

The corollary is that the economies of the older cities might rejuvenate themselves by converting from declining manufacturing to growing services- and information-related activities. Consider, for example, a newspaper account of a 1978 address by the geographer Jean Gottman on such global administrative centers as London, Paris, New York, and Toronto: "The world city has become not a production machine but an information machine in the broadest possible sense.... *Thus the world city revitalizes itself.*"[28]

While alluring, this path to urban rejuvenation may yield less than meets the eye—especially if the eye sees only downtown sites. It is true that a high national growth rate makes the idea sound plausible; the city's manufacturing losses then slow or cease, and services employment tends to rise. But over the course of the business cycle, the older metropolis's cyclical job gains have in practice been largely offset by its cyclical losses, notably in its manufacturing sector.[29]

In turn, the older area's industrial stagnation has exposed its central city to the full brunt of job suburbanization. In long-term perspective, then, the conversion to a services orientation after 1945 seems to have occurred almost by default. In practice, conversion has been tantamount to contraction for the older city.

THE PRIMACY OF THE SEEDBED FUNCTION

And yet one element in the foregoing conversion scenario has considerable validity. That is the notion of market-generated urban economic rejuvenation. In the course of the 1960s, in fact, a number of writers came to emphasize precisely the process through which urban economies "adapt" to economic change by restructuring themselves away from declining or decentralizing industries.

27. Melvin W. Webber, "The Post-city Age," *Daedalus*, 97:4 (Fall 1968), as reprinted in *Internal Structure of the City*, ed. Larry S. Bourne (New York: Oxford University Press, 1971), pp. 498–499.

28. Edward J. Logue, paraphrasing Gottman, as quoted in Ian Menzies, "Is Boston Really a Hub of Universe?" *Boston Globe*, 27 November 1978. Emphasis added.

29. See Chapter 5, pp. 103–112.

Thus far, we have implicitly regarded technological innovations as working in a single, decentralizing fashion. Now it is time to recognize that innovation can also be a source of industrial replenishment for aging economies, whether urban or national in scale.

The older cities—and their larger metropolitan areas, and with them the Manufacturing Belt as a whole—were not merely passive victims of technological change. They were also the setting in which innovations were generated. As Chapter 6 will show, the Manufacturing Belt's producers traditionally enjoyed something of a monopoly on innovative capacity. Apart from the decentralizing influence of specific innovations, then, there is also a more general technological dimension to consider: the capacity *to spawn and to hold the economy's new industries.*

So the question becomes one of how a city's cycle of growth and decline is linked to the birth and expansion of new industries. In landmark studies, Raymond Vernon, Benjamin Chinitz, Allen Pred, Wilbur Thompson, and Jane Jacobs concluded that this "seedbed" capacity was the key to a city's economic position.[30] As high-wage, heavily unionized locations, the older urban areas were inevitably vulnerable to the flight of their mature industries to the economy's low-wage areas beyond the heartland. The seedbed function provided a means of countering such industrial dispersion, through a continuing replenishment of the local industrial base.

From this perspective, it seems clear that any established area's economic position depends on *the balance between aging and rejuvenation*—that is, *between dispersive and replenishing tendencies.* Throughout most of this century, innovative capacity enabled the industrial metropolis to counter obsolescence through a process of continuing industrial rejuvenation. Most of the older areas—and with them the Manufacturing Belt as a whole—thus managed to replace their dying or migrating industries with new and expanding ones.

30. Raymond Vernon, *Metropolis 1985* (Cambridge: Harvard University Press, 1960), ch. 5; Benjamin Chinitz, *City and Suburb: The Economics of Metropolitan Growth* (Englewood Cliffs, New Jersey: Prentice-Hall, 1964), pp. 17–22; Allen R. Pred, *The Spatial Dynamics of U.S. Urban-Industrial Growth, 1800–1914* (Cambridge: MIT Press, 1966), chapter 3; Wilbur Thompson, "The Economic Base of Urban Problems," in *Contemporary Economic Issues,* ed. Neil W. Chamberlin (Homewood, Illinois: Irwin, 1969), pp. 6-9; and Jane Jacobs, *The Economy of Cities* (New York: Random House, 1969).

The virtual industrial collapse of the Manufacturing Belt in the decade after 1966 suggests that it can no longer rely on the seedbed function for such rejuvenation. The reasons for this historical shift are obviously complex. An explanation to be offered later focuses on regional resource endowments and the role they have played in attracting the new industrial sources of innovation, notably electronics and petrochemicals. But whatever the exact explanation, the decentralization of the seedbed function probably signals irreversible changes in the economy's regional structure, and a sharply diminished economic role for the older city.

2

MEASURING URBAN LEGACIES

By our definition, the fundamental urban problem is one of nineteenth-century cities in a late-twentieth-century economy, where such cities serve as processing centers for the minority poor. In this view, the old city's diminishing job opportunities and its continuing use as a kind of reservation threaten to create a permanent urban underclass.

This fundamental urban problem results in part from the city life-cycle: the tendency for old cities to decline after World War II, while young cities continue to grow. Accordingly, Chapter 2 provides an overview of urban legacies. We begin with a definition of city age, then relate a city's age to its region, and close with a look at the key policy issue.

DEFINING CITY AGE

The first task is to derive an index of city age that can capture a city's developmental legacy (economic and political) in a logically consistent way. Insofar as large American cities can be viewed as *industrial artifacts,* a city's effective age may depend on its technological premises—a product of the historical epoch within which the settlement first reached great size.

Here we can benefit from Borchert's list of the broad technological epochs shaping American urban development.[1] The critical point in this succession is 1920, the beginning of Borchert's "auto–air–amenity" epoch. Following his lead, we might ask which of today's largest cities experienced their formative development before 1920. In other words, from among the 30 largest cities in 1970, which were catapulted to great size by the pre-World War I industrialization? And which experienced their initial large-scale development only after the industrial revolution and mass immigration had come to an end?

CITY AGE AND THE TIMING OF METROPOLITAN DEVELOPMENT

This question should be recast to refer to the development of the 30 cities' larger metropolitan areas. One effect of such an adjustment is to focus (as per Thompson's insight) on urban "labor market pools," regardless of jurisdictional lines.[2] Another is to recognize that the placement and flexibility of city borders are themselves variables to be explained. Hence, measuring age by the timing of the legal city's growth may obscure as much as it reveals.

A convenient year for comparing the relative sizes of the 30 metropolitan areas is 1910, the last census year before World War I. For spatial units to approximate the 30 areas, we can draw upon the Census Bureau's initial (1950) metropolitan area definitions. These earliest SMSA definitions typically included far fewer counties than do more recent ones, and, therefore, provide better spatial approximations to the actual 1910 settlements.[3]

Table 2-1 ranks the 30 settlements according to their 1910 populations. From among the 30, the dozen that were then largest can be termed "old," or (equivalently) "industrial," in keeping with their

1. John R. Borchert, "American Metropolitan Evolution," *Geographical Review,* 57 (1967), pp. 301–332.

2. Wilbur Thompson, "Economic Processes and Employment Problems in Declining Urban Areas," in *Post-Industrial America: Metropolitan Decline & Inter-Regional Job Shifts,* eds. George Sternlieb and James W. Hughes (New Brunswick: Center for Urban Policy Research, 1975), p. 189.

3. The population sizes of these constant-area settlements are listed for each census year between 1900 and 1950 in the first appendix table of Donald J. Bogue, *Population Growth in Standard Metropolitan Areas: 1900–1950* (Washington, D.C.: U.S. Government Printing Office, 1953).

TABLE 2-1
1950 Employment Structure and Post-1950 City and SMSA Growth

Age class	City, by 1910 metropolitan size	Percentage of urbanized-area work force in manufacturing, 1950	Percentage change in city population, 1950–1975	Percentage change in SMSA population, 1970–1975
Industrial	New York	30.8	− 5	− 3.4
	Chicago	37.7	− 14	+ 0.1
	Philadelphia	35.6	− 12	− 0.6
	Boston	28.7	− 21	+ 1.7
	Pittsburgh	38.0	− 32	− 3.6
	St. Louis	33.8	− 39	− 1.7
	San Francisco	19.4	− 14	+ 1.6
	Baltimore	30.9	− 10	+ 3.2
	Cleveland	40.5	− 30	− 4.3
	Buffalo	39.7	− 30	− 1.6
	Detroit	46.9	− 28	+ 0.2
	Cincinnati	33.4	− 18	− 0.2
Anomalous	Los Angeles	25.6	+ 38	− 1.4
	Washington	7.4	− 11	+ 3.6
	Milwaukee	42.9	+ 4	+ 1.6
	Kansas City	24.5	+ 3	+ 1.0
	New Orleans	15.6	− 2	+ 4.6
	Seattle	19.8	+ 4	− 0.9
Young	Indianapolis	33.1	+ 67	+ 3.2
	Atlanta	18.3	+ 32	+13.2
	Denver	16.8	+ 17	+13.3
	Columbus	25.0	+ 42	+ 5.8
	Memphis	20.5	+ 67	+ 4.7
	Nashville	22.9	+143	+ 7.7
	Dallas	18.4	+ 87	+ 7.3
	San Antonio	11.6	+ 89	+10.0
	Houston	21.4	+123	+14.9
	Jacksonville	13.1	+162	+12.7
	San Diego	15.7	+131	+16.9
	Phoenix	10.4	+522	+25.4
Means and significance of mean differences				
Industrial cities		34.6	− 21	− 0.7
Young cities		18.9	124	11.3
Difference		15.7	145	12.0
Significance		$p < .001$	$p < .01$	$p < .001$

Sources: Column 1: U.S. Bureau of the Census, *1950 Census of Population, Vol. II, Characteristics of the Population, United States Summary.* Column 2: Same as for Table 1-1. Column 3: U.S. Bureau of the Census, *Current Population Reports,* Series P-25, No. 709, September 1977.

roles as focal centers for the industrial revolution. Conversely, the dozen then having small populations can be described as "young," since their main development came only later. Between these are six cities (Los Angeles, Washington, Milwaukee, Kansas City, New Orleans, and Seattle) that might be labeled "anomalous," in the sense that their development is not easily ascribed to either period.

Our index of city age follows naturally. For the rest of this study, the central cities of the older (or industrial) urban areas will be described as old, or industrial, the central cities of the younger areas will be termed young, and those of the six anomalous areas will be deemed anomalous. In short, we have measured the ages of the metropolitan areas of today's 30 largest cities, then labeled the 30 cities accordingly.[4]

DEVELOPMENTAL LEGACIES: ECONOMIC AND POLITICAL

The age classification captures differences in urban industrial endowments fairly well. As background, it might be noted that 1950 represents a natural benchmark from which to measure city growth, because the decade of the 1950s was the first to show widespread central-city population declines.

In 1950, the "industrial" urban areas had characteristically high work-force shares in the manufacturing sector, and the younger areas had characteristically low shares. As Table 2-1 shows, the older areas averaged 35%, versus less than 20% for the younger ones. (As is indicated in the table, this difference in class means is statistically significant at a probability value of .001.[5]) Judging by urban economic structure, then, the developmental legacies of younger and older areas remained sharply drawn in the years just after World War II.[6]

---

4. For a critical analysis of the logic of the age approach, see the appendix to this chapter.

5. While the results of such t-tests are reported throughout the study, as derived from equally sized classes under the assumption of unequal variances, such results cannot be construed as measuring differences in means from randomly drawn samples. The two primary age-classes are not samples. By hypothesis, they are small populations. The probability values reported for differences in means are thus presented merely as indicators of the reliability (in a nonrigorous sense) of the hypothesized classification scheme.

6. For simplicity, little if anything will be said in the study about the anomalous cities. As a purely impressionistic note, it might be suggested here at the outset that Seattle, Kansas City, and Los Angeles (in effect the "first young city") behave more like young

The age classification fits the pattern of city growth and decline perfectly. The clarity of the fit may be seen in the rest of Table 2-1, which describes city and metropolitan growth rates. *Between 1950 and 1975 every "old" city lost population and every "young" one grew.* During the first half of the 1970s, a matching pattern of growth and decline emerged among younger and older metropolitan areas.

Institutional Endowments

The life-cycle growth pattern has political as well as economic sources. Putting it more generally, urban developmental legacies are institutional as well as technological. Indeed, the evidence suggests two divergent models of city–suburban interaction.

City–suburban social cleavages are more pronounced in the industrial areas. Average city *incomes* in 1974 fell sharply below those of suburban households in old areas—but not, as a rule, in young ones (Table 2-2). Instead, young cities tended to have average incomes that equal or exceed those of suburban households.

Table 2-2 shows that such differences have been matched by contrasts in city–suburban political interaction. In particular, the *boundaries* of the old cities have long been frozen. By contrast, every young city has annexed large amounts of new land since 1950. As a result, young cities typically enjoy larger land areas and include more of the urban population.

The result for measured city growth-rates, of course, is that young cities would appear to grow faster than old, even if growth within constant boundaries were the same. There is a second, more practical consequence of these systematic differences in city annexation power. It stems from the fact that city borders are a key variable for metropolitan fiscal organization.

The divergent political legacies of young and old cities translate today into differing city *fiscal environments*. By virtue of their large-scale annexations, some young cities have become functional approximations of "metro" governments. On the other hand, the governments of the tightly bounded old cities have been especially vulnerable to fiscal distress. The list of fiscally suspect big-city gov-

---

cities, and Washington, New Orleans, and Milwaukee, more like old ones. The trouble with such an observation is that, for the anomalous cities, relative to young or old ones, economic and political legacies are less clearly aligned with each other.

TABLE 2-2
Indicators of City–Suburban Political Separation (Percentages)

Age class	City, by 1910 metropolitan size	Income per capita in 1974: city–SMSA ring ratio	1950–1975 change in municipal land area
Industrial	New York	77	0
	Chicago	78	7
	Philadelphia	83	1
	Boston	82	0
	Pittsburgh	93	2
	St. Louis	81	0
	San Francisco	101	2
	Baltimore	80	0
	Cleveland	68	1
	Buffalo	83	5
	Detroit	80	0
	Cincinnati	96	4
Anomalous	Los Angeles	100	3
	Washington	na	0
	Milwaukee	83	90
	Kansas City	91	292
	New Orleans	92	0
	Seattle	111	18
Young	Indianapolis	100	580
	Atlanta	85	256
	Denver	104	70
	Columbus	89	338
	Memphis	118	169
	Nashville	109	2208
	Dallas	111	176
	San Antonio	75	279
	Houston	101	206
	Jacksonville	119	2436
	San Diego	108	225
	Phoenix	100	1499
	Class means		
Industrial cities		84	2
Young cities		102	704
Difference		18	702
Significance		$p < .001$	$p = .02$

Sources: Column 1: Raw income data are from the second source for Table 1-1. Estimated ratios are based on interpolated city population figures. Except for city–counties, 1974 city population figures are interpolated from 1973 and 1975 figures appearing in U.S. Bureau of the Census, *Statistical Abstract of the United States* for 1976 and 1977. For city–counties, the population source is the same as for Table 2-1, Column 3.

TABLE 2-3
Big Cities with Poor Bond Ratings in March, 1976

Cities with bond ratings below Moody's Aa	
New York	New Orleans
Philadelphia	Jacksonville
Detroit	Pittsburgh
Baltimore	Buffalo
Cleveland	Newark

Source: John Craig and Michael Koleda, "The Future of the Municipal Hospital in Major American Cities" (processed, April 1976), using data from *Moody's State and Municipal Yearbook, 1975,* and weekly supplements 1975–1976, Moody's Investor Service, New York, New York.

ernments, as gauged by municipal bond ratings midway through the 1970s, is thus heavily dominated by the industrial cities (Table 2-3).

In sum, the indicators trace out a strikingly clear-cut set of contrasts as between young and old cities. Consider the list: (*a*) initial industrial structure, (*b*) subsequent city and metropolitan growth, (*c*) city-suburban political separation, and (*d*) city fiscal position. Each seems to divide consistently between those cities whose formative development preceded World War I and those whose main growth has come more recently.[7]

The next point to consider is that urban legacies also differ systematically *by region*—and in particular, between the Manufacturing Belt and the rest of the nation.

THE REGIONAL DIMENSION

A great deal of attention has gone to the Sunbelt–Snowbelt issue, the so-called "Second War between the States." But the mechanism driving such regional realignments may actually operate via the system of cities. As a demographer writes concerning the politics of regional population shifts, *"This 'tournament of the belts' is a kind of preliminary bout to the main event—the tension between growing and declin-*

---

7. The appendix to this chapter focuses on the potentially circular link between a city's annexation power and the age class to which it has been assigned.

ing cities."[8] The basis for this view is that regional economic shifts pivot on the industrial metropolis and the rising younger urban area of the periphery.

THE REGIONAL STRUCTURE OF THE CITY LIFE-CYCLE

As noted in Chapter 1, young and old cities are typically located in different regions. The point is illustrated in Figure 2-1, which maps out the distribution of the 24 urban settlements in 1910—the year that serves as the touchstone for our age taxonomy. Since urban development of a region typically awaited its industrialization, the nation's largest settlements were then heavily concentrated within the Manufacturing Belt. In terms of our age labels, all the "old" cities but San Francisco therefore lie in the core region today. And all the young ones but Columbus and Indianapolis lie outside it.

This correspondence means that life-cycle realignments inevitably register as regional shifts as well. Hence it is by no means surprising that a massive research effort assessing the economic plight of the Northeast should single out the region's "mature" metropolitan areas. The problem of the industrial metropolis, in other words, was seen as the key to any strategy for *Revitalizing the Northeastern Economy:*

> The primary locus of the present structural problems in the Northeastern economy is in the mature urban areas. . . . Therefore, an economic revitalization strategy in the Northeast must contain components addressed to the special problems of these mature urban areas.[9]

In the same light, it is easy to understand why perceptions of the urban problem (and hence of welfare reform, and of city fiscal relief) should vary so starkly by region. Insofar as young cities are characteristic of the South and West, the industrial periphery may not have a distinct and clearly defined urban problem.

That is not to say that the South and West are somehow less burdened than the Manufacturing Belt by poverty. *But poverty is a separate issue, one that can be addressed through nonspatial policies.* At the same time, of course, the very vitality of most young cities proba-

---

8. Peter Morrison, "Current Demographic Changes in Regions of the United States" (Santa Monica: Rand, 1977), p. 3.

9. The Academy for Contemporary Problems, *Revitalizing the Northeastern Economy—An Action Survey* (Columbus, Ohio: 1977), p. 33.

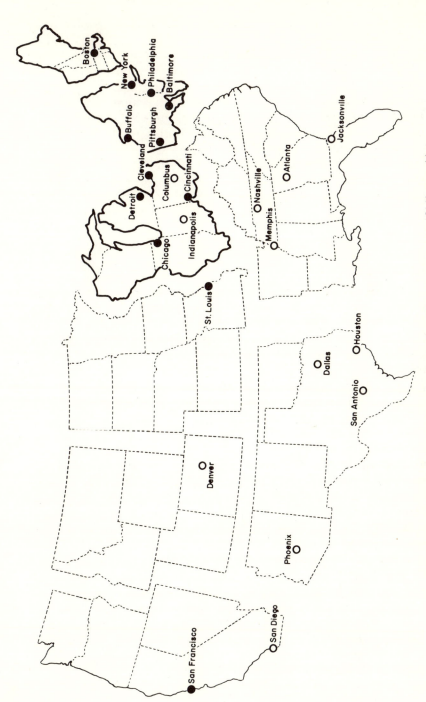

Figure 2-1. The regional clustering of the old cities. (●) Industrial cities; (○) Young cities.

bly bolsters the view widespread in the South and West that since anyone who "wants to work" can find a job, no new poverty measures are needed.

In any case, it will be suggested later that the regional divergence in interests and perceptions is likely to persist, and not fade away. If so, the prospect is one of continuing regional conflict, marked by concentrations of the minority poor in the ghettos of the industrial cities, linked in turn in a network spanning the old industrial heartland. Some plausible federal responses to this prospect are noted in the next section.

JOBS TO PEOPLE OR PEOPLE TO JOBS?

At issue is the continuing concentration of the minority poor in cities offering diminishing job opportunities, that is, in the declining industrial cities. This fundamental urban problem has two distinct sources: the old city's long-term job losses and its concentrated minority poverty, as reinforced by suburban exclusionary practices. The two combined perpetuate large-scale structural unemployment, with its attendant pathologies.

Insofar as the residual role of the industrial city is indeed as a reservation for the minority poor, one federal response can obviously be no response. As noted in Chapter 1, this laissez-faire approach might be termed a reservation strategy—the strategy implicit in the "benign neglect" of the Nixon and Ford years. While the reservation approach was seen as a coherent response to the urban problem, we noted that in the long run it is also a high-risk proposition, since it contains the seeds of future urban crises. Consequently, this book focuses on the feasibility of two other federal options, each of which would aim to reduce structural unemployment and to restore the upgrading process.

The first, a *rejuvenation* strategy, would attempt to restore the old city's job base. To have much effect, this jobs-to-people approach would have to be mounted on a fairly large scale, perhaps approximating the urban Marshall Plan that is sometimes proposed. Like the reservation strategy, it would sanction the spatial quarantining of the poor. But, through a politically administered plan for the old city's economic redevelopment, it would also attempt to enhance their job skills and to stabilize their employment patterns.

By contrast, a *dispersal* strategy would write off the old city as an economic center, but would also reject its use as a reservation. This people-to-jobs option would encourage the gradual redistribution of the minority poor to areas of rapid job growth, including both the suburban locations now effectively closed to them and the South and West generally. A variant of this approach, confined to the scale of the metropolis, has been described as a "disinvestment" strategy.[10] Its corollary is the "planned shrinkage"—or, more accurately, the *balanced* shrinkage—of the industrial cities.[11]

THE NO-GROWTH MOVEMENT AND THE URBAN POOR

In the short run, political considerations come down decisively on the side of rejuvenation—if not complete inaction (i.e., the reservation strategy). Such considerations go beyond the exigencies of the decentralized federal system, in which political representatives vie for federal aid for their particular bailiwicks, regardless of circumstances. Also present are complex cross-currents of environmental, preservationist, and antipoor sentiments.

The complex motives behind the new no-growth arguments are well illustrated in recent comments by Colorado's Governor Lamm:

> We're bumping the limits of finite resources out in the West. To add endless sprawl, air pollution, water consumption in the West doesn't make any sense. *I don't want everybody from Boston, Newark, Detroit moving to Colorado.* It aggravates our problem, it aggravates theirs [italics added].[12]

The reference to Boston, Newark, and Detroit is revealing. Changing the names to Columbus, Phoenix, and Seattle would change the meaning of the passage, freeing it of the specter of the minority poor.

The question, then, is not whether dispersal would be politically preferred to a rejuvenation strategy. Instead, the key issue is *whether, in the long run, a rejuvenation strategy can have much impact on the underlying economic trajectories of the industrial cities.* As a first step

10. William G. Colman, *Cities, Suburbs, and States* (New York: Free Press, 1975).

11. See, for example, Roger Starr, "Making New York Smaller," *The New York Times Magazine,* 14 November 1976, pp. 32 *et seq.*

12. Quoted in Neal R. Peirce, "Bringing Jobs to People," *Dallas Times Herald,* 26 February 1978.

in assessing this issue, the next chapter surveys the demographic dimensions of the city life-cycle.

APPENDIX: THE POTENTIAL BIAS IN THE CITY AGE CLASSIFICATION

In devising an index of city age, I began with the 30 largest cities—legal cities—as of the last census year, 1970. The aim was to design an age index that might capture the political and economic effects of the timing of their initial large-scale development. Following Birch and Thompson, I chose to use the urban areas of the 30 cities as the units whose growth should be traced.

There were two reasons for such a decision. First, the unit whose development I wished to date was, in fact, the entire urban (or metropolitan) area—as a local economy or labor market pool. Second, city annexation power is itself a variable. Any measure of city age that refers to the growth of the legal city is sure to be distorted by differences in annexation power among cities. (About which, more momentarily.)

Accordingly, I measured and ranked the 1910 population sizes of the 30 urban areas. From within this list, the dozen largest were deemed old; the dozen smallest, young; and the rest, anomalous—neither young nor old. Using this classification, I then found a series of tight age-class contrasts for a variety of urban indicators.

BORDERS AND BIAS IN THEORY AND PRACTICE

Did any step in this sequence bias the empirical results that were obtained? The answer is maybe. In starting from a list of the largest legal cities in 1970, I naturally included cities like Nashville and Jacksonville, whose recent mergers with their counties have added considerably to their populations, thereby helping to propel them onto the 30-largest list. Though less dramatically evident, the issue is similar for other young cities, all of which have registered large annexations since World War II.

Such young cities would thus seem to be on the list in the first place because of their recent annexation-based growth. If so, it is hardly surprising to find that "young" cities have an easier time annexing new territory than old ones. In short, there is an element of undeni-

TABLE 2-4

Correlates of Population Growth in the 30 Largest Cities: 1950–1975
(Percentage Changes)

Age class	City, by 1910 metropolitan size	City population	SMSA population[a]	City territory
Industrial	New York	− 5	5	0
	Chicago	− 14	35	7
	Philadelphia	− 12	31	1
	Boston	− 21	54	0
	Pittsburgh	− 32	5	2
	St. Louis	− 39	32	0
	San Francisco	− 14	46	2
	Baltimore	− 10	47	0
	Cleveland	− 30	29	1
	Buffalo	− 30	22	5
	Detroit	− 28	40	0
	Cincinnati	− 18	35	4
Anomalous	Los Angeles	+ 38	67	3
	Washington	− 11	97	0
	Milwaukee	+ 4	41	90
	Kansas City	+ 3	49	292
	New Orleans	− 2	54	0
	Seattle	+ 4	67	18
Young	Indianapolis	+ 67	58	580
	Atlanta	+ 32	104	256
	Denver	+ 17	128	70
	Columbus	+ 42	69	338
	Memphis	+ 67	50	169
	Nashville	+143	50	2208
	Dallas	+ 87	110	176
	San Antonio	+ 89	80	279
	Houston	+123	142	206
	Jacksonville	+162	93	2436
	San Diego	+131	185	225
	Phoenix	+522	267	1499
Mean and significance of mean differences				
Industrial cities		− 21	32	2
Young cities		124	111	704
Difference		145	80	702
Signficance		$p < .01$	$p < .01$	$p = .02$

Source: Same as for Table 1-2.

[a] 1975 SMSA territorial definitions have been used to measure 1950 as well as 1975 SMSA population.

able circularity in the relationship linking a city's annexation power, its measured growth, and its age.

Nevertheless, in practice, the impact this bias has had on the indicators is insignificant, because, by no coincidence, *cities with large-scale annexations after 1950 also invariably had rapidly growing urban areas.* As Table 2-4 shows, between 1950 and 1975 city annexation power and rapid urban growth went together, just as did frozen city borders and sluggish areawide growth rates. As joint developmental outcomes, annexation and urban growth are thus closely linked. Hence, none of the young cities has grown rapidly and to large size only because of its annexation power.

So a valid theoretical objection can be made to the age index. But as a practical matter, the classification remains a reliable and broadly consistent measure of the timing of a city's formative development. And the key question remains: Why should economic and political legacies diverge so clearly with the timing of development?

3

WHY CITY GROWTH RATES DIFFER

Between 1950 and 1975, the young cities gained 4 million new residents, and about doubled in aggregate population (Figure 3-1). During the same period, the industrial cities lost a roughly comparable number of people. Whereas the growing young cities tended to experience proportionate increases by race, the industrial cities underwent sharp changes in their racial (and, hence, income) strucutres.

The proximate causes of such realignments can be specified with some precision. In this chapter, city population changes will be treated as outcomes generated by three distinct influences: (*a*) decentralization, (*b*) annexation, and (*c*) urban-area growth. More specifically, a city's growth is said to depend on the degree to which annexation and rapid urban growth *counter* the tendency toward white suburbanization.

As can be seen in Table 3-1, aggregate growth contrasts reflect nearly uniform city-by-city tendencies for the period of 1950–1970, after which the pattern for individual young cities becomes more variegated. Accordingly, the first section develops a statistical test of how the three influences interacted between 1950 and 1970 to determine growth rates in the 30 cities. The second section makes use of the statistical technique to show why decline has precipitated such

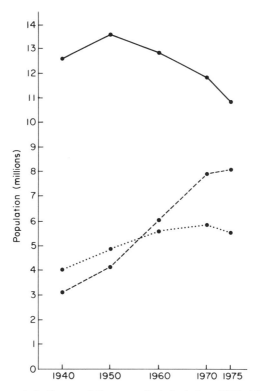

Figure 3-1. Aggregated city population growth trajectories, 1940–1975. (——) 11 Industrial cities (New York excluded); (–––) 12 Young cities (· · ·) 6 Anomalous cities.

pronounced racial shifts. The concluding section brings the story up to date with an overview of the cross-currents of the 1970s—and in particular of the no-growth metropolis, whose appearance has meant accelerated population losses by the old cities.

ACCOUNTING FOR CONTRASTS IN CITY POPULATION GROWTH

Contrasts in city growth rates between 1950 and 1970 have two obvious explanations. First, and as a definitional matter, the incorporated land areas of some cities were greatly expanded, while those of others remained unchanged. Second, the urban settlements contain-

TABLE 3-1

Population (in Thousands) of the 30 Largest Cities, 1940–1975

Age class	City, by 1910 metropolitan size	1940	1950	1960	1970	1975
Industrial	New York	7455	7892	7782	7895	7482
	Chicago	3397	3621	3550	3367	3099
	Philadelphia	1931	2072	2003	1949	1816
	Boston	771	801	697	641	637
	Pittsburgh	672	677	604	520	459
	St. Louis	816	857	750	622	525
	San Francisco	635	755	740	716	665
	Baltimore	859	950	939	906	852
	Cleveland	878	915	876	751	639
	Buffalo	576	580	533	463	407
	Detroit	1623	1850	1670	1511	1335
	Cincinnati	456	504	503	453	413
Anomalous	Los Angeles	1504	1970	2479	2816	2727
	Washington	663	802	764	757	712
	Milwaukee	587	637	741	717	666
	Kansas City	399	457	476	507	473
	New Orleans	495	570	628	593	560
	Seattle	368	468	557	531	487
Young	Indianapolis	387	427	476	745	715
	Atlanta	302	331	487	497	436
	Denver	322	416	494	515	485
	Columbus	306	376	471	540	536
	Memphis	293	396	498	624	661
	Nashville	167	174	171	448	423
	Dallas	295	434	680	844	813
	San Antonio	254	408	588	654	773
	Houston	385	596	938	1233	1327
	Jacksonville	173	205	201	529	535
	San Diego	203	334	573	697	774
	Phoenix	65	107	439	582	665
	Class totals					
11 Industrial cities[a]		12,614	13,601	12,865	11,898	10,845
12 Young cities		3,153	4,205	6,016	7,906	8,142
6 Anomalous cities		4,017	4,905	5,644	5,921	5,624

Source: Same as for Table 1-1.

[a] Excluding New York.

ing the 30 central cities grew at widely varying rates. As one would expect, a central city's measured population growth naturally reflected each of these influences.

Table 3-2 documents the association between the two variables and city population changes. As regards annexation, the table discloses that population losses occurred only in cities with constant borders—the industrial cities and Washington, D.C. Conversely, the large population gains accruing to young cities accompanied substantial increases in city territory. Measured city growth rates thus varied predictably with changes in municipal land area.

But the table also reveals a pattern of correlation between city and urban-area growth rates. Urban growth rates ranged much higher in young than in industrial areas over the two decades. The fastest-growing of the older urbanized areas (San Francisco) lagged behind the slowest-growing younger one (Indianapolis). And the 1950–1970 mean rate of 124% for the younger areas was more than triple the mean for the older ones. Here, then, is a second apparent source of city growth contrasts.

DECENTRALIZATION AND ITS OFFSETS

Since both factors appear to penalize old cities and favor young ones, their relative influences remain unclear. We can get a more specific reading on their roles by regressing city growth rates on the two explanatory variables taken together.

For the period 1950–1970, define the variable CG as the percentage change in a city's population. Let CG be a linear function of UG, the percentage growth of the city's urbanized area, and of L, the percentage increase in the city's incorporated territory. The "sample," of course, consists of the 30 largest cities in 1970.[1]

By an ordinary-least-squares regression,

$$CG = -61.9 + 1.1UG + 0.06L, \qquad (1)$$
$$(6.1) \quad (10.0) \quad (5.6)$$
$$N = 30, \qquad SE = 32.3, \qquad R^2 = .88.$$

---

1. The statistical caveat offered in the last chapter should be repeated here. Except from a time-series perspective, the values of variables for the 30 cities should not be viewed as samples. The 30 cities constitute the *population* of the nation's largest cities. It follows that the assumptions underlying the least-squares estimators are not being met.

TABLE 3-2

Correlates of Population Growth in the 30 Largest Cities, 1950 – 1970
(Percentage Changes)

Age class	City, by 1910 metropolitan size	City population	Urbanized-area population	City territory
Industrial	New York	0	32	0
	Chicago	− 7	36	7
	Philadelphia	− 6	38	0
	Boston	− 20	19	0
	Pittsburgh	− 23	20	2
	St. Louis	− 27	34	0
	San Francisco	− 8	60	0
	Baltimore	− 5	36	0
	Cleveland	− 18	42	1
	Buffalo	− 20	36	5
	Detroit	− 18	49	0
	Cincinnati	− 10	36	4
Anomalous	Los Angeles	+ 43	109	3
	Washington	− 6	93	0
	Milwaukee	+ 12	51	90
	Kansas City	+ 11	64	292
	New Orleans	+ 4	46	0
	Seattle	+ 14	102	18
Young	Indianapolis	+ 74	63	587
	Atlanta	+ 50	131	256
	Denver	+ 24	110	42
	Columbus	+ 44	80	242
	Memphis	+ 58	64	108
	Nashville	+157	73	2208
	Dallas	+ 94	148	137
	San Antonio	+ 60	72	165
	Houston	+107	140	171
	Jacksonville	+159	118	2436
	San Diego	+108	177	219
	Phoenix	+444	300	1350
	Class means			
Industrial cities		− 14	37	2
Young cities		115	123	676
Difference		128	86	674
Significance		$p < .001$	$p < .001$	$p < .01$

Sources: Column 1: Same as the first source listed for Table 1-1. Columns 2 and 3: U.S. Bureau of the Census, *1950 Census of Population, Vol. I, Number of Inhabitants, United States Summary;* and *U.S. Census of Population: 1970, Number of Inhabitants [Final Report PC(1)-A1], United States Summary.*

Fully 88% of the variation in city growth rates can thus be explained by city annexation differences and by differential urban growth.

The negative constant indicates that a city for which both the annexation and the urban growth variables equalled zero would have lost more than half its 1950 population by 1970. On the average, each 1% increase in the urban growth rate (UG) raised a city's growth by 1.1 percentage points above this loss. Surprisingly, a 1% expansion in city territory (L) raised the predicted growth rate by a mere .06 percentage points. Small as this latter coefficient seems, the parenthetical t-ratios (the absolute values of the ratios of the estimates to their standard errors) indicate that all three estimates are statistically significant.

The regression easily fulfills the conventional criteria for a good statistical fit. But does it really say anything new about city growth?

The Constant as an Index of Suburbanization

Despite its apparent simplicity, the regression is open to varying interpretations. A skeptic might contend that of course cities will share in the growth of their larger areas, if only because, definitionally, they form major components of those areas. And the terms of such participation should naturally improve if the city can annex peripheral land, where growth should be greatest.

This view is not so much wrong as it is fragmentary. It ignores a critical aspect of the fitted regression: the enormous negative constant of −61.9%. It would thus seem to yield an incomplete, and so perhaps misleading, assessment of the equation.

To disregard the constant is to overlook the enormous impact suburbanization has had on city growth rates. Once again, the constant estimates the change in city population when the two explanatory variables are statistically equated to zero. Hence it shows the predicted rate of change for a fixed-territory city (one for which $L = 0$) in a no-growth metropolis (one for which $UG = 0$). The "prediction," of course, is that a city in such circumstances would have lost 61.9% of its initial population during the two decades.

The reason this huge decline can be read as an index of suburbanization follows from the definition of the constant. Under the assumptions just described, the urban area neither grows *nor declines*. Therefore whatever population the city loses must be exactly compensated by gains in the rest of the area, that is, in the city's suburbs. In this sense, the constant tells how much of our hypothetical city's population was (hypothetically) lost to its suburbs between 1950 and 1970.

Rapid Urban Growth as an Offset to Dispersion

The negative constant depicts the tendency toward the scattering of the city's population beyond its borders. By the same token, the *positive* coefficients describe offsets to such decentralization. The coefficient estimate for the urban growth (*UG*) variable of 1.1%, for example, means that an areawide growth rate of about 57% should have sufficed to keep a fixed-territory central city from losing population. By the same token, higher rates of urbanized-area expansion should have stimulated positive city growth.[2]

Figure 3-2 portrays this interplay between urban growth and dispersion. The figure renders a "partial" regression line, one based on only two of the three coefficient estimates in Eq. (1). The line relates city to urban population growth rates on the assumption that municipal land area remained constant during the period. Since it reflects only the constant and the urban-growth coefficient, city territory is implicitly taken as a fixed parameter.

The constant of −61.9% becomes the graph's y-intercept. In this case, the intercept refers to the fitted city growth rate when urban growth is equated to zero. From the intercept, the line of average relationship rises at a rate of 1.1 percentage points for each 1% increase in the independent variable *UG*. Now we can reinterpret the points made a moment ago, supplementing them here with the graph.

The diagram shows that city population losses occur at a diminishing rate, until the areawide growth rate reaches about 57%, at which point the line crosses x-axis. For higher rates of urban growth (and we saw in Table 3-2 that they reached as high as 300%), positive city growth will take place. Above the critical value of 57%, each percentage point of urban growth will raise the city's growth rate by about the same amount—all without annexation.

---

2. In terms of the standard urban density function, the offset relationship can be interpreted as an upward shift of the entire curve so as to damp the effects on centralized population of a falling density gradient (γ). For historical estimates of the two parameters (the height of the curve and its shape), see Edwin S. Mills, *Studies in the Structure of the Urban Economy* (Baltimore: Johns Hopkins Press, 1972), chapter 3.

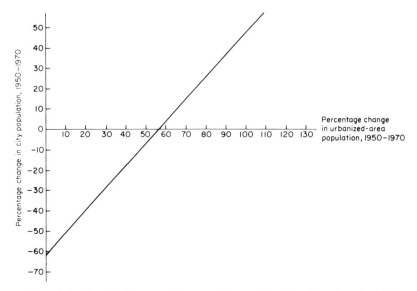

Figure 3-2. Rapid urban growth as an offset to dispersion. [Based on Eq. (1).]

Making Sense of the Annexation Coefficient

What about the annexation coefficient? While it seems obvious that the annexation variable should provide a second major offset to population dispersion, we would expect it to have a far larger impact than the regression indicates. The coefficient estimate of .06% means that each 100% increase in a city's 1950 land area added, on average, 6 percentage points to the city's population growth over the decade.

What are we to make of this seemingly trivial coefficient estimate? Perhaps the key explanation is that it refers only to the experiences of the cities that actually annexed new territory during the two decades, that is, not to any of the industrial cities. Our expectations of a greater impact are almost certainly predicated on the image of the older metropolis, an image that posits large residential concentrations within a short distance of the city. But this image has no connection whatsoever with the regression estimate, because the old cities registered virtually no territorial expansion during the period covered. In other words, the coefficient estimate is entirely unaffected by the *potential* increment to population that might have resulted from a purely hypothetical industrial-city annexation.

For the young cities (the ones that count, statistically) there are two general reasons that the annexation coefficient should be so low. First, the estimate would be considerably larger if it were attached to the only explanatory variable in the regression. But it shares part of the statistical credit with the urbanized-area growth variable, with which it is highly correlated. Second, and more to the point, young-city annexations have usually been *preemptive,* carried out in anticipation of future residential and commercial development.

One indication of the significance of preemptive annexation can be seen in Table 3-3, which reports census estimates of "rural" land within the actual borders of some young cities. As a rule, the vacant land taken in during an annexation will loom larger the bigger the annexation. This tendency is particularly clear in the enormous territorial expansions that followed from two recent city–county consolidations in Nashville and Jacksonville—which in 1970 found, respectively, 34 and 55% of their land areas classified as rural.

From the standpoint of fitting a least-squares regression to observed data, we can begin to see why the annexation coefficient is so small. These larger annexations are likely to give the statistical appearance of tiny territorial elasticities of population growth. And the nature of the "offset" to population dispersion comes to appear

TABLE 3-3
Rural Territory within the Borders of Eight Large "Extended" Cities, 1970[a]

City, by size of rural share	Rural share of total city area (%)	Square miles of "rural" city land	Total city land area (square miles)
New Orleans	56	111	197
Jacksonville	55	422	766
Nashville	34	174	508
San Diego	33	104	317
Kansas City	24	77	316
Memphis	18	40	217
Houston	8	37	434
Indianapolis	7	28	379

Source: Same as the first source listed for Table 1-1.

[a]"An extended city contains one or more areas, each of at least 5 square miles in extent and with a population density of less than 100 persons per square mile according to the 1970 census. The area or areas constitute at least 25 percent of the land area of the legal city or total 25 square miles or more." [U.S. Bureau of the Census, *U.S. Census of Population: 1970, Number of Inhabitants,* p. ix.]

somewhat less direct, since the offset factor will fully come into play only in the several decades following the redefinition of the city's borders.

In short, both annexation and rapid urban growth may be viewed as counteracting the decentralization of city population. We can develop this interpretation further by fitting out each city's predicted growth rate and comparing that with its actual performance.

Table 3-4 lists fitted and actual values (and their differences, the residuals) for the 30 cities. The table provides specific illustrations of how urban growth and annexation offset (or fail to offset) the tendency toward surburbanization. The city of Detroit, for example, lost 18% of its 1950 population between 1950 and 1970. Its urbanized area grew by 49% while its land area remained unchanged. So against the decentralization factor of −62%, the computed offset of 55% (i.e., 1.1 × 49) leaves a predicted deficit of −7%. Since the actual loss was −18%, the residual is −11.

At the other end of the scale, Dallas's 94% gain was based on urban growth of 148% and a 137% increase in city territory. Accordingly, the offsets to the tendency toward decline were more potent, adding up to 174%. The equation thus assigns Dallas a value of 112%, leaving a residual (using unrounded numbers) of −17%.

Why City Growth Rates Differ

In sum, city growth rates differ because the impact of dispersion has varied with city annexations and with urban growth rates. The life-cycle incidence of gains and losses in city population thus has clear and specific sources. Both annexation and urban growth have assumed high values in young cities, and low values in old ones. Hence decentralization has exacted a much greater toll on the industrial cities than on the central cities of younger urban areas.

THE DEMOGRAPHIC TRANSFORMATION OF THE OLD CITY

From a policy standpoint, the problem with city population losses is that they have been racially selective. If decline were demographically

TABLE 3-4
Fitted and Actual Values for the Basic City Growth Regression (Percentage Changes)[a]

Age class	City, by 1910 metropolitan size	Residual: Actual − Fitted			Offset effects	
					Urban growth	Annexation
Industrial	New York	+27	0	− 27	36	0
	Chicago	+15	− 7	− 22	40	0
	Philadelphia	+15	− 6	− 20	43	0
	Boston	+22	− 20	− 42	21	0
	Pittsburgh	+16	− 24	− 40	22	0
	St. Louis	− 3	− 27	− 24	38	0
	San Francisco	−13	− 8	+ 5	67	0
	Baltimore	+18	− 5	− 22	40	0
	Cleveland	− 2	− 18	− 16	47	0
	Buffalo	+ 2	− 20	− 22	40	0
	Detroit	−11	− 18	− 7	55	0
	Cincinnati	12	− 10	− 22	40	0
Anomalous	Los Angeles	−16	+ 43	+ 59	122	0
	Washington	−47	− 6	+ 41	104	0
	Milwaukee	+13	+ 12	0	57	5
	Kansas City	−15	+ 11	+ 27	72	18
	New Orleans	+15	+ 4	− 11	52	0
	Seattle	−39	+ 14	+ 52	114	1
Young	Indianapolis	+31	+ 74	+ 44	71	35
	Atlanta	−49	+ 50	+ 99	147	15
	Denver	−39	+ 24	+ 63	123	3
	Columbus	+ 2	+ 44	+ 42	90	15
	Memphis	+31	+ 58	+ 26	72	18
	Nashville	+ 5	+157	+152	82	132
	Dallas	−17	+ 94	+112	166	8
	San Antonio	+33	+ 60	+ 27	81	10
	Houston	+ 3	+107	+104	157	10
	Jacksonville	−57	+159	+216	132	146
	San Diego	−40	+108	+148	198	13
	Phoenix	91	+444	+353	336	81

[a] Based on Eq. (1).

"balanced," then the industrial cities could reasonably be viewed as moving to new equilibrium positions, that is, to sizes better suited to their diminishing roles within the national and world economies. Adjustments would, of course, be required of firms, urban landowners, and city governments. But the descent to a smaller size could proceed without enormous dislocations.

This scenario of balanced decline has little, if any, relevance to the depopulation of the industrial city. As is well known, population losses have precipitated sharp changes in the old city's demographic structure. In categorical terms, whites left the industrial cities in large numbers after 1950, and were replaced, in part, by black and Spanish-speaking newcomers.

SELECTIVE ABANDONMENT, BALANCED GROWTH

The exodus from the industrial cities after 1950 was therefore much larger than their net population losses might suggest. The average old city lost about 15% of its total population between 1950 and 1970, but white declines ran considerably higher. Judging by the median figure in Table 3-5, one in three of the typical old city's 1950 whites was gone by 1970. Since a fair number of the "remaining" two-thirds were in reality Spanish-speaking newcomers, the rate of exodus among non-Spanish-speaking whites was greater still. As a rough approximation, then, the typical industrial city lost *between one-third and one-half* of its English-speaking white population during the two decades.

By contrast, the median young city had two-thirds *more* whites in 1970 than in 1950. Such white increases did tend to lag behind increases in the young city's nonwhite population. Nevertheless, growth rates for whites and for population totals were fairly similar. As one illustration of this tendency, the dozen young cities had an average white increase of 112%, a figure close to the average total gain of 115%.

Racial Shifts and City–Suburban Income Contrasts

City–suburban income ratios in 1970 varied directly with 1950–1970 growth rates for city whites. The racially transformed old cities had predictably low average household incomes relative to those in their suburbs. Specifically, as Table 3-5 shows, the mean value for the 12 older SMSAs in 1970 was only .77. By the same token, central-city incomes actually exceeded those of suburban households in most younger SMSAs. As if to highlight the racial connection, the few exceptions to this rule (Atlanta, Denver, and San Antonio) each experienced unusually low white growth between 1950 and 1970. Where

TABLE 3-5

Population Changes by Race in the 30 Largest Cities, 1950–1970 (Percentage Changes)

Age class	City, by 1910 metropolitan size	Percentage change in population, 1950–1970		Average household income: city–SMSA ring ratio: 1970
		Whites	Nonwhites	
Industrial	New York	− 15	138	66
	Chicago	− 29	128	73
	Philadelphia	− 34	348	75
	Boston	− 31	172	69
	Pittsburgh	− 31	30	89
	St. Louis	− 48	67	70
	San Francisco	− 26	151	81
	Baltimore	− 34	88	65
	Cleveland	− 40	96	65
	Buffalo	− 33	161	105
	Detroit	− 46	122	82
	Cincinnati	− 24	62	85
Anomalous	Los Angeles	+ 24	204	92
	Washington	− 60	92	95
	Milwaukee	− 2	391	73
	Kansas City	− 2	106	81
	New Orleans	− 17	48	86
	Seattle	+ 5	146	81
Young	Indianapolis	+ 67	113	107
	Atlanta	+ 15	111	89
	Denver	+ 15	210	89
	Columbus	+ 33	117	118
	Memphis	+ 52	66	104
	Nashville	+200	63	129
	Dallas	+ 66	281	102
	San Antonio	+ 58	91	70
	Houston	+ 92	161	104
	Jacksonville	+209	67	—
	San Diego	+ 96	321	98
	Phoenix	+441	490	103
Means and significance of mean differences				
Industrial cities		− 33	130	77
Young cities		112	174	101
Difference		145	44	24
Significance		$p < .001$	$p = .33$	$p < .001$

Sources: Columns 1 and 2: Same as for Table 3-2, Columns 2 and 3. Column 3: "1970 Survey of Buying Power," *Sales Management* (10 June 1971), as reported in Advisory Commission on Intergovernmental Relations, *City Financial Emergencies: The Intergovernmental Dimension* (Washington, D.C.: U.S. Government Printing Office, 1973).

white increases were at or above the median rate for the young cities, city incomes matched or surpassed suburban ones.

In sum, the industrial city's demographic transformation between 1950 and 1970 stemmed in large part from the massive exodus of its white population. Both young and old cities attracted large numbers of nonwhites after 1950, but only the old cities experienced major changes in their racial structures. Moreover, a city's *income* position relative to its suburban ring varied accordingly. So by this reading, the change in a city's white population constituted a key outcome.

MIGRATION, SUBURBANIZATION, AND CITY RACIAL SHIFTS

Why did white growth rates diverge so decisively between young and old cities? In general, central-city racial shifts reflected three broad influences. Young cities annexed large amounts of peripheral territory, where whites have been concentrated; old cities did not. Second, whites decentralized in much larger numbers than blacks. Finally, black and white migrants to and among urban areas differed in their choices of metropolitan destinations. These three influences will now be examined more closely.

Whites' Preferences for Younger Urban Areas

The younger urbanized area's rapid growth between 1950 and 1970 was based on proportionate increases in its white *and* nonwhite populations. In a strikingly uniform pattern, younger areas experienced white growth apace with the growth of their total populations. This racial balance is epitomized by the exact equality of the average increases for whites and for total population. As Table 3-6 illustrates, each indicator averaged 123% for the dozen younger areas.

By contrast, the white populations of most industrial urban areas grew at rates well below the national increase. Specifically, the average gain for the 12 old cities was 26%, compared with a 32% rise in the number of whites in the nation as a whole. Hence the older area's white population growth can be attributed to natural increases alone—that is, to the excess of births over deaths. To put it another way, the typical industrial metropolis experienced *no net influx of whites* from the rest of the nation between 1950 and 1970.

TABLE 3-6

Urbanized-Area Growth Rates for Whites and Total Population, 1950–1970

Age class	City, by 1910 metropolitan size	Percentage increase in urbanized-area population, 1950–1970	
		Whites	Total
Industrial	New York	20	32
	Chicago	23	36
	Philadelphia	29	38
	Boston	15	19
	Pittsburgh	19	20
	St. Louis	26	34
	San Francisco	34	60
	Baltimore	23	36
	Cleveland	31	42
	Buffalo	28	36
	Detroit	38	49
	Cincinnati	33	36
Anomalous	Los Angeles	96	109
	Washington	83	93
	Milwaukee	41	51
	Kansas City	54	64
	New Orleans	40	46
	Seattle	95	102
Young	Indianapolis	56	63
	Atlanta	140	131
	Denver	105	110
	Columbus	76	80
	Memphis	63	64
	Nashville	80	73
	Dallas	140	148
	San Antonio	70	72
	Houston	134	140
	Jacksonville	143	118
	San Diego	166	177
	Phoenix	303	300
Means and significance of mean differences			
Industrial cities		26	37
Young cities		123	123
Difference		96	86
Significance		$p < .001$	$p < .001$

Source: Same as for Table 3-2, Columns 2 and 3.

Decentralization as a White Phenomenon

The absence of net white migration to the older metropolis undoubtedly contributed to the selective abandonment of the industrial city. But it represents only part of the explanation. The rest involves (*a*) the rates at which blacks and whites decentralized, and (*b*) the old city's fixed boundaries.

The statistical specification introduced earlier can help us work out the influence of each factor. To this end, racially disaggregated versions of the growth equation have been estimated and are reported in Table 3-7. The results suggest that the initial regression masked two contrary tendencies—one for whites, another for blacks. The regression for whites alone reveals an even higher rate of dispersion than characterized the total population. Conversely, the regression for blacks discloses no tendency whatsoever toward decentralization.

The comparison can be rendered more incisively in a diagram. Figure 3-3 depicts two partial regression lines—one for city and area whites, the other for city and area nonwhites. As in the earlier diagram, the annexation variable has been suppressed as a fixed parameter. And once again, the *y*-intercept corresponds to the index of dispersion.

Here the line for city whites strongly resembles the total-population line presented in Figure 3-2. The *y*-intercept equals −67%. The "offset" provided by the areawide change in whites (i.e., the urban-growth coefficient) is now an even 1.0. On average, *an area's white population therefore had to grow by two-thirds of its 1950 size just to keep the number of central-city whites from declining.* Accordingly, the line for

TABLE 3-7
City Growth Regressions for Whites and Nonwhites (Percentage Changes)

Dependent variable	$\hat{B}_0$	$\hat{B}_1$	(Urbanized-area growth, by race)	$\hat{B}_2$	(Municipal territory)	R^2
City whites	−67.2 (6.6)	1.0 (8.3)	(urbanized-area whites)	0.08 (6.5)	(annexation)	.89
City nonwhites	8.9 (0.3)	0.9 (6.4)	(urbanized-area nonwhites)	0.02 (1.2)	(annexation)	.60
Total city population	−61.9 (6.1)	1.1 (10.0)	(urbanized-area total)	0.06 (5.6)	(annexation)	.88

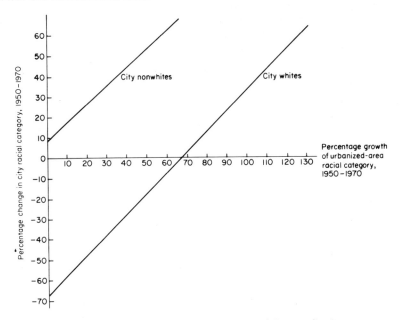

Figure 3-3. Contrasts by race in the pace of decentralization.

whites crosses the x-axis at an areawide growth rate of 67%. Above that threshold, a city would have gained whites even without annexation. Fully 10 of the younger areas (along with those containing Los Angeles, Seattle, and Washington) did, in fact, register gains in whites above the 67% mark. Not one of the dozen older areas came close.

The regression line for nonwhites discloses an opposite pattern. Since the constant estimate fails to differ significantly from zero, it appears that virtually all nonwhite increases in urbanized-area population resulted from increases within central cities themselves. Nor is the annexation coefficient statistically significant. On both counts, the evidence summarized in Table 3-7 suggests a reversal of the causal ordering. If anything, central-city gains in nonwhites "determined" areawide increases, not the other way around.

Urban Growth, Suburbanization, and White Abandonment

So it is clear why young cities gained whites and old cities lost them in such large numbers. The explanation pivots on the tendency toward large-scale white decentralization within urban areas. In view of this tendency, what actually happened depended on (a) the number of white migrants entering a particular urban area and on (b) the central city's annexation power.

From this standpoint, the sources of the young cities' continued white gains are easy to specify. Their urban areas registered substantial net white inmigration, some of which translated into white increases within initial central-city borders. In addition, city boundaries were expanded to include rapidly developing peripheral territory, where white population growth was highest. In combination, the two factors more than offset the tendency toward white decentralization.

By contrast, the end of net white migration to the older metropolis after 1950 exposed the industrial city to the full brunt of white decentralization. Since every old city's borders were frozen, decentralization translated directly into suburbanization. In short, *massive white suburbanization in urban areas receiving no net influx of whites*—this was the reason for the old city's racial transformation between 1950 and 1970.

The 1950s and 1960s can thus be viewed as a time of transition for the industrial cities—a period in which age-correlated demographic shifts were especially well defined. But what of the 1970s? From the standpoint of the larger issue, rejuvenation versus dispersal, we need to track life-cycle growth tendencies into the more recent past.

LIFE-CYCLE TENDENCIES IN THE 1970s

Many see the demographic upheavals of the 1970s as abrupt breaks from past modes of urban development. On some counts that may be an accurate perception. Yet the no-growth metropolis, the increased migration to the Sunbelt, and even the population losses hitting some young cities are each tendencies that can be explained within the framework we have established so far. This concluding section brings the record up to date and focuses on some key empirical questions that have surfaced in the late 1970s concerning the positions of the industrial cities.

THE NO-GROWTH METROPOLIS

In the regressions reported earlier, the large negative constants were said to represent indexes of suburbanization. They were statistical estimates of the population losses fixed-territory cities would have incurred had their urban areas failed to grow. Since all 30 areas did grow, the no-growth metropolis remained only a statistical construct. And so did the index: No city lost anything like 60% of its 1950 population.

In the first half of the 1970s, the no-growth metropolis became a reality. As Figure 3-4 shows, the national birth rate fell dramatically after 1970. This reduction gave migration flows a new strategic significance in the determination of urban growth rates. As Peter Morrison writes, "The fall-off in the birth rate has . . . revealed migratory comings and goings as the principal determinant of local growth and decline."[3]

Such "comings and goings" were directed, on balance, away from the industrial metropolis. As Table 3-8 shows, none of the dozen younger areas lost population between 1970 and 1975. With all but two receiving a net influx of people, their average gain exceeded 11%. Meantime every older SMSA but San Francisco experienced a net outmigration, and the average older area actually lost population.

THE REDUCTION IN CITY GROWTH RATES

After 1970, as areawide population growth slowed, city growth rates diminished across the board (Table 3-9). Most young cities managed to maintain their population sizes between 1970 and 1975 (although Atlanta, with a huge 12% loss, is a notable exception). But the average change for the old cities was a 9% loss, a figure that works out to about triple the rate of decline for the preceding 20-year period.

We can place these accelerated losses in perspective by reestimating the growth equation for the 5-year period, 1970–1975:

$$CG = -8.6 + 0.6UG + 0.3L, \tag{2}$$
$$(7.8) \quad (4.6) \qquad (3.4)$$
$$N = 30, \quad SE = 5.0, \quad R^2 = .66.$$

As might be expected, the equation's explanatory power has fallen off for this shorter interval. But the specification still accounts for some

---

3. Peter Morrison, "Current Demographic Changes in Regions of the United States" (Santa Monica: Rand, 1977), p. 2.

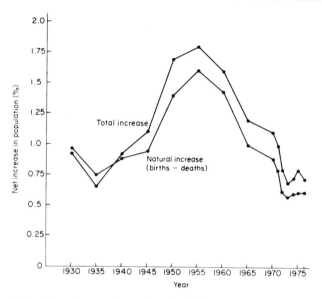

Figure 3-4. Annual rates of growth in the U.S. population, 1930–1976.

two-thirds of the variation in growth rates, and the *t*-ratios indicate highly significant coefficient estimates.

According to the equation, a typical fixed-territory city in a no-growth metropolis lost 9% of its 1970 population between 1970 and 1975. And that is precisely what the average industrial city did lose over the 5-year interval. It might also be noted that the 20-year equivalent of the suburbanization index (i.e., the regression constant) is −39%, or somewhat lower than the −62% we estimated (less accurately) from 1950 to 1970 data.

GENTRIFICATION, BLACK FLIGHT, AND DOWNTOWN REVIVAL

The reduction in SMSA and city growth rates in the first half of the 1970s resulted not only from a falling birth rate, of course, but also from the deepest recession to hit the United States since the 1930s. Reaching an unemployment rate of 9% nationally in 1975, the recession ravaged the economies of the industrial cities. But it passed, giving way to a relative improvement in the economic positions of most old cities.

TABLE 3-8
Gains and Losses in SMSA Population, 1970–1975

Age class	SMSA, by size in 1910	Percentage change in SMSA population, 1970–1975	Net migration (percent) 1970–1975
Industrial	New York	− 3.4	− 5.4
	Chicago	+ 0.1	− 3.7
	Philadelphia	− 0.6	− 2.9
	Boston	+ 1.7	− 0.4
	Pittsburgh	− 3.6	− 4.5
	St. Louis	− 1.7	− 4.9
	San Francisco	+ 1.6	− 1.4
	Baltimore	+ 3.2	+ 0.5
	Cleveland	− 4.3	− 7.0
	Buffalo	− 1.6	− 3.6
	Detroit	+ 0.2	− 3.9
	Cincinnati	− 0.2	− 3.7
Anomalous	Los Angeles	− 1.4	− 5.1
	Washington	+ 3.6	− 1.1
	Milwaukee	+ 1.6	− 1.7
	Kansas City	+ 1.0	− 3.0
	New Orleans	+ 4.6	− 0.2
	Seattle	− 0.9	− 3.7
Young	Indianapolis	+ 3.2	− 1.4
	Atlanta	+13.2	+ 7.3
	Denver	+13.3	+ 8.3
	Columbus	+ 5.8	+ 1.0
	Memphis	+ 4.7	− 0.5
	Nashville	+ 7.7	+ 3.7
	Dallas	+ 7.3	+ 1.7
	San Antonio	+10.0	+ 2.8
	Houston	+14.9	+ 8.1
	Jacksonville	+12.7	+ 7.6
	San Diego	+16.9	+12.4
	Phoenix	+25.4	+19.3
	Class means		
Industrial cities		− 0.7	− 3.4
Young cities		11.3	5.9
Difference		12.0	9.3
Significance		$p < .001$	$p < .01$

Source: Same as for Table 1-2, Column 3.

TABLE 3-9

Correlates of City Growth, 1970–1975 (Percentage Changes)

Age class	City, by 1910 metropolitan size	City population	SMSA population	City territory
Industrial	New York	− 5	− 3	0
	Chicago	− 8	0	0
	Philadelphia	− 7	− 1	0
	Boston	− 1	+ 2	0
	Pittsburgh	−12	− 4	0
	St. Louis	−16	− 2	0
	San Francisco	− 7	+ 1	0
	Baltimore	− 6	+ 3	0
	Cleveland	−15	− 4	0
	Buffalo	−12	− 2	0
	Detroit	−12	0	0
	Cincinnati	− 9	0	0
Anomalous	Los Angeles	− 3	− 1	0
	Washington	− 6	+ 4	0
	Milwaukee	− 7	+ 2	0
	Kansas City	− 7	+ 1	0
	New Orleans	− 6	+ 5	0
	Seattle	− 8	− 1	0
Young	Indianapolis	− 4	+ 3	0
	Atlanta	−12	+13	0
	Denver	− 6	+13	20
	Columbus	− 1	+ 6	28
	Memphis	+ 6	+ 5	29
	Nashville	− 5	+ 8	0
	Dallas	− 4	+ 7	16
	San Antonio	+18	+10	43
	Houston	+ 8	+15	13
	Jacksonville	+ 1	+13	0
	San Diego	+11	+17	2
	Phoenix	+14	+25	10
	Class means			
Industrial cities		− 9	− 1	0
Young cities		2	11	13
Difference		11	12	13
Significance		$p < .01$	$p < .001$	$p < .01$

Sources: Column 1: same as Table 1-1, second source. Column 2: same as for Table 1-2, Column 3. Column 3: same as for Table 1-2, Column 2, second source.

As the recovery extended into 1979, media observers began to write of an "urban renaissance."[4] Its hallmarks were increasing downtown prosperity, "gentrification" (i.e., an influx of childless, young, middle-class professionals to inner-city neighborhoods), and a modest movement of middle-class blacks to the suburbs. Such tendencies testify to a welcome resiliency on the part of a least some of the industrial cities. But they tell us little if anything about the outlook for the minority poor.

First, the migration of the minority poor away from the manufacturing belt during the 1970s has been miniscule. In fact, until about 1975 there was no perceptible outflow at all. Then, between 1975 and 1977, it appears that some 200,000 people with incomes below the poverty line left the belt for the South and the West.[5] In relation to the recession's cataclysmic impact, this seems a surprisingly limited response: New York City alone is said to have lost fully 600,000 private-sector jobs between 1969 and 1978.[6] Moreover, the 200,000 who left includes rural as well as urban migrants, white as well as minority poor.

Second, the scale of black suburbanization remains rather limited. It is said that the number of suburban blacks rose by one-third between 1970 and 1977. But this increase brought the black share of the suburban population to only 6% in the latter year, much of which was concentrated in older suburban cities that were themselves declining.[7] A more accurate assessment of this issue must, of course, await the 1980 Census. But what is clear is that a sizable black and Spanish-speaking underclass remained behind in the deteriorating outer neighborhoods of the industrial cities.

4. See T. D. Allman, "The Urban Crisis Leaves Town," *Harper's*, December 1978, for the most overstated version of the case; more persuasive essays are "A City Revival?" in *Newsweek*, 15 January 1979, pp. 28–35, and Blake Fleetwood, "The New Elite and an Urban Renaissance," *The New York Times Magazine*, 14 January 1979, pp. 16 *et seq.* Allman also claims that Newark, the extreme case, "is in the midst of an impressive social, economic, and cultural revival that is confounding the prophets of urban decay," "Newark Defies the Prophets of Doom," *In These Times*, 10–16 January 1979, p. 4.

5. An estimate based on Robert Reinold, "Poor People Migrating to South in Reversal of a Historic Pattern," *New York Times*, 4 December 1978, which in turn summarizes Larry H. Long, "Interregional Migration of the Poor: Some Recent Changes," Bureau of the Census, Series P-23, No. 73, December 1978.

6. Peter J. Solomon, New York's Deputy Mayor for Economic Development, as reported in "Solomon Predicts Zero Increase in Employment in New York City," *New York Times*, 13 January 1979.

7. *Newsweek*, 15 January 1979, p. 30.

This divergence in conditions within the industrial cities themselves has been incisively portrayed by the columnist George Will, writing about New York:

> Today there are three New Yorks. One is a small Manhattan oasis of corporate headquarters, tourism, entertainment, advertising. Another is the fragile and declining city of the industrial working class. The third is the necropolis, the growing stalking corpse symbolized by (but not limited to) the South Bronx.[8]

From the vantage point of the late 1970s, it seems evident that urban death is real—not for old cities per se, but for specific neighborhoods within them. It is of interest that the conservative Will recommends that the federal government assist in the relocation of the residents of such dying neighborhoods: "*Federal policy should aid the contraction of the city by subsidizing the movement of people* to regions with enough vitality to absorb them."

APPENDIX: CLEVELAND'S HISTORICAL LIFE-CYCLE

The term "life-cycle" suggests that individual cities occupy differing segments along their long-term growth trajectories. One writer, Jay W. Forrester, has designed an intertemporal simulation model capable of tracking out a hypothetical city's long-term growth and decline—a model from which Forrester has inferred brutal policy guidelines.[9]

Such inferences are hard to take seriously, because the Forrester model is irrelevant to actual city growth. Among other things, his simulations assume (*a*) constant city territory and (*b*) no urban development beyond a city's legal borders. In other words, the legal city and the urban area are made definitionally coterminous and are locked into a constant land area. If the diverse records of the 30 largest cities yield any single lesson, however, it is the strategic significance of a city government's ability to extend its borders so as to encompass new development at the periphery.

This appendix illustrates the point through an historical case-study of one industrial city, Cleveland. The results suggest that the advent of the automobile made annexation a functional prerequisite to the

8. *Newsweek*, 8 January 1979, p. 72.
9. Jay W. Forrester, *Urban Dynamics* (Cambridge: MIT Press, 1969).

continued growth of any tightly bounded, densely settled industrial city.

MODELING CLEVELAND'S GROWTH AND DECLINE

Cleveland makes a particularly good subject for this sort of historical case study. Through most of the urban area's history, the legal city's domain was repeatedly shifted outward, apace with the peripheral growth of the physical city. (Table 3-10 shows, for example, that over the century before 1930, the city's borders were shifted outward in every decade but the 1880s; after 1930, significant annexation came to an abrupt halt.) The fact that the legal city's territorial growth proceeded gradually and in small steps means that we have numerous observations with which to fit a life-cycle specification. As for the other explanatory variable, the urban-area growth rate, we can use the growth of the two counties, Cuyahoga and Lake, that constituted the Census Bureau's (1950) original definition of the Cleveland SMSA.

Switching to an historical perspective does, however, require changes in the treatment of the city's annexation activity. An exact counterpart to the earlier equations would make the decennial percentage change in Cleveland's population depend only on the rate of urban growth and the amount of land annexed during the decade. But exploratory tests indicate that better results can be obtained with one additional variable, a variable measuring the land annexed in the immediately *preceding* decade. Along with urban growth (UG, as before) and current period annexation (L), I will therefore include a lagged version of the annexation variable, calling it L_{-1}.

The resulting specification explains 84% of the decade-to-decade variation in Cleveland's growth over the 12 decades between 1850 and 1970:

$$CG = -24.9 + 1.2UG + 0.3L + 0.4L_{-1}, \qquad (3)$$
$$(1.6) \quad (2.4) \qquad (1.3) \quad (2.8)$$
$$N = 12, \qquad SE = 24.0, \qquad R^2 = .84.$$

By this reading, one might conclude that the end of the city's growth after 1930 resulted simply from reductions in the rates of municipal annexation and urban growth.

Any such interpretation is open to question, however, because even the best of the four estimates lies on the borderline of statistical sig-

TABLE 3-10
Correlates of Cleveland's Historical Growth and Decline

| | Cleveland's population at the end of the decade (thousands) | Percentage change during the decade | | |
| | | Cleveland's population | Population of Cuyahoga and Lake Counties | Municipal territory |
Decade				
1850s	43	155	49	36
1860s	93	114	58	64
1870s	160	73	44	134
1880s	261	63	54	0
1890s	382	46	40	22
1900s	561	47	43	34
1910s	797	42	47	23
1920s	900	13	28	25
1930s	878	−2	2	3
1940s	915	4	16	2
1950s	876	−4	23	0
1960s	751	−14	7	0

Source: R. D. McKenzie, *The Metropolitan Community* (New York: McGraw-Hill, 1933), pp. 336–340; and U.S. Bureau of the Census, decennial censuses of population since 1880.

nificance. In other words, all the estimates are accompanied by relatively high standard errors. In contrast to the earlier, cross-sectional regressions, then, this one raises as many questions as it answers.

THE AUTO AGE AND THE END OF CLEVELAND'S GROWTH

One source of the uncertainty surrounding Eq. (3) could be that the structural relationship governing Cleveland's growth changed during the period considered. Then the estimates in the equation would, in reality, reflect composites of the true parameters prevailing at different periods in the city's development. With so few statistical observations to go on, however, we cannot explore this possibility without additional, but available, information. In his 1933 work, *The Metropolitan Community*, R. D. McKenzie related Cleveland's measured growth to the city's territorial expansion and described the individual growth trajectories of a series of roughly concentric areas within the expanding legal city.[10] For our purposes, the main implication of his account

10. R. D. McKenzie, *The Metropolitan Community* (New York: McGraw-Hill, 1933), chapter 11.

is that Cleveland's spatial development did in fact shift from a centralized to a dispersed pattern.

Specifically, McKenzie's raw data disclose that the year 1920 marked a watershed in the city's development. During the 1920s, with the construction of the first extensive urban highway networks, the spatial constraints on the area's development were decisively loosened. After 1920, the city would have to continue to annex large amounts of new territory at the periphery to grow at all, as the shift in settlement patterns undercut the population growth of the incorporated city.

These remarks are based on the evidence in Figure 3-5, which reproduces and updates one of McKenzie's diagrams. One thing the figure shows is that the growth trajectory etched out by decennial census counts is actually the envelope of a whole series of constant-territory growth curves. More to the point, the diagram reveals that *during the 1920s, for the first time, the inner and older 80% of the land area within the city was already losing population.* After 1920, only compensating growth in the most recently annexed territorial band kept the city as a whole from declining.

Figure 3-6 allows us to get behind these aggregate changes and to trace the growth behavior of seven different belts annexed in various decades between 1840 and 1920. Each belt had a given population at the time it was annexed. Each then grew at very high but decelerating rates for several decades. (Since the graphs have semilog scales, the flattening slopes for each curve are accurate reflections of the deceleration.) Perhaps the main point of the diagram is that every individual belt added to the city before 1900 had ceased to grow by the 1920s. For the most populous belt (the one added in the decade before 1880), this shift seems particularly telling, coming as it did after a decade of very rapid growth.

As a sidelight on the Cleveland regression, the data underlying these diagrams reveal why the lagged annexation coefficient proved more powerful (and more consistent) a predictor of the city's growth than the unlagged one. (The data are presented in Table 3-11.) The reason is that the major development in each annexed area took place after its annexation by the city. Once the partly settled area was brought within the corporate city, it could receive the utility services that the city government alone could provide. Then and only then could full residential development proceed.

By way of illustration, Table 3-11 shows that when first brought within the city's borders, the seven annexed belts displayed gross resi-

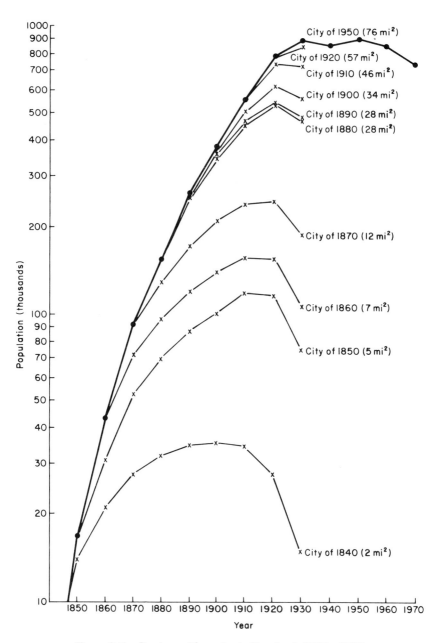

Figure 3-5. Fixed-area life-cycles in Cleveland: 1840–1970.

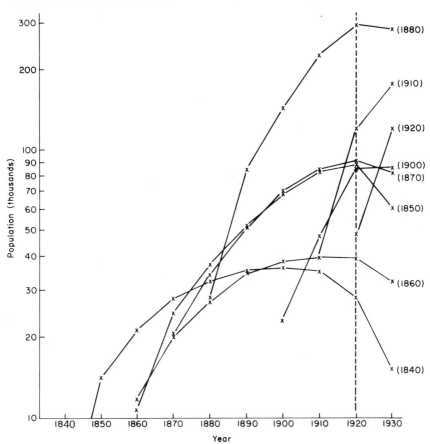

Figure 3-6. Growth behavior of eight concentric zonal areas in Cleveland: 1850–1930.

dential densities of 3000 to 4000 persons per square mile. But within two or three decades, their densities soared to between 15,000 and 20,000. And the time of fastest growth was invariably the first full decade after annexation—precisely the one specified by the lagged annexation variable. To repeat, then, the regression's annexation coefficients behave as they do because annexation anticipated (and may have been a prerequisite to) full residential development.

In sum, McKenzie's evidence is consistent with the findings of urban historians that until World War I, city governments actually facilitated urban development by annexing undeveloped areas and

TABLE 3-11

Growth Behavior of Seven Concentric "Belt" Areas in Cleveland, 1840–1930

Percentage growth of the area's population during the decade before	City of 1840	"Belt" annexed during decade before						
		1850	1860	1870	1880	1900	1910	1920
1850	*134*[a]							
1860	49	*292*						
1870	33	*133*	72					
1880	15	52	˃ 36	*71*				
1890	9	40	29	53	*200*			
1900	2	30	9	34	*70*			
1910	−1	23	4	20	58	*99*		
1920	−19	7	−1	9	30	73	*194*	
1930	−46	−32	−18	−9	−3	6	47	*152*
		Average density (persons per square mile)						
1. First census after annexation	3,200	800	6,000	4,300	1,700	3,800	3,500	4,400
2. Peak	19,100	25,800	20,500	19,700	18,300	13,900	15,200	11,100
Year of peak density	1900	1920	1910	1920	1920	?	?	?

Source: Same as first source listed for Table 3-10.

[a] Italicized rates designate the belt registering the highest percentage increase for the corresponding decade.

TABLE 3-12
1920–1950 Population Growth of Major Fixed-Territory Cities

City, by rate of growth	Percentage growth of city population, 1920–1950	Percentage growth of 1950 SMSA, 1920–1950	Constant land area (square miles)
Boston	7	24	46
St. Louis	11	48	61
Philadelphia	14	35	128
Buffalo	14	45	41
Baltimore	29	57	78
New York	40	52	300
New Orleans	47	66	196
San Francisco	53	122	45
Washington	53	156	61

Source: Same as for Table 3-10; and Donald J. Bogue, *Population Growth in Standard Metropolitan Areas: 1900–1950* (Washington, D.C.: U.S. Government Printing Office, 1953).

providing them with essential utility services.[11] By the 1920s, however, the centralized industrial city had given way to the decentralizing industrial metropolis.[12] Technological changes originating as far back as the 1880s had coalesced to create a new locational regime, one freeing plants and residences from previously binding ties to central sites.

Thus annexation became vital to the city's continued growth. When Cleveland's large-scale annexations stopped after 1930, the crest of the wave of urban growth left the city in its wake. For Cleveland, as for such other tightly cities as Boston, Buffalo, Philadelphia, and St. Louis, the end of annexation brought the end of the city's growth (see Table 3-12).

But why, after nearly a century of regular annexations, did annexation come to an end in Cleveland, and in the other industrial cities? This question is addressed in Chapter 4.

11. See, for example, Blake McKelvey, *American Urbanization: A Comparative History* (Glenview, Illinois: Scott, Foresman, 1973), p. 111.

12. The term "centralized industrial city" is probably accurate in relation to the decentralization that would come after 1920, but it should be noted that when decentralization is defined rigorously (as the reduction through time in an urban area's density gradient), the process seems to have been in effect as far back as the data reach, that is, since 1880. See Mills, *Studies,* pp. 48–49.

4

CITY BORDERS AND THE TIMING OF URBAN DEVELOPMENT

Since the late 1940s, a central city's annexation power has varied consistently with the timing of its economic development.[1] Cities that reached large size early in the century have lost the power to expand their municipal boundaries. Accordingly, the industrial metropolis has become deeply divided along city–suburban lines, lines encircling a politically isolated and territorially contained central city. By contrast, in urban areas that have developed more recently, central-city governments have continued to expand their territories. As Table 4-1 shows, a number of young cities have thus retained substantial administrative hegemony over their larger urban areas.[2]

1. For an authoritative overview of the city annexations between 1950 and 1970, see Richard L. Forstall, "Changes in Land Areas for Larger Cities," *The Municipal Yearbook: 1972* (Chicago: International City Management Association, 1972), pp. 84–87. Studies of variations in annexation power among cities include David G. Bromley and Joel Smith, "The Historical Significance of Annexation as a Social Process," *Land Economics,* 49 (August 1973), pp. 294–309; Thomas R. Dye, "Urban Political Integration: Conditions Associated with Annexation in American Cities," *Midwest Journal of Political Science,* 8 (November 1964), pp. 430–446; Kenneth T. Jackson, "Metropolitan Government versus Suburban Autonomy: Politics on the Crabgrass Frontier," in *Cities in American History,* eds. Kenneth T. Jackson and Stanley K. Schultz (New York: Alfred A. Knopf, 1972), pp. 442–462; and Leo F. Schnore, *The Urban Scene: Human Ecology and*

TABLE 4-1
City Annexation Power and City Territorial Coverage

Age class	City, by 1910 metropolitan size	Percentage change in city land area, 1950–1975	Central city's percentage share of 1970 urbanized-area population	City land area Jan. 1, 1976 (square miles)
Industrial	New York	0	49	300
	Chicago	7	50	223
	Philadelphia	1	49	128
	Boston	0	24	46
	Pittsburgh	2	28	55
	St. Louis	0	33	61
	San Francisco	2	27	45
	Baltimore	0	57	78
	Cleveland	1	38	76
	Buffalo	5	43	41
	Detroit	0	38	138
	Cincinnati	4	41	78
Anomalous	Los Angeles	3	34	464
	Washington	0	30	61
	Milwaukee	90	57	95
	Kansas City	292	54	316
	New Orleans	0	62	197
	Seattle	18	45	84
Young	Indianapolis	580	91	375
	Atlanta	256	42	131
	Denver	70	49	114
	Columbus	338	68	173
	Memphis	169	94	280
	Nashville	2208	100	508
	Dallas	176	63	309
	San Antonio	279	85	264
	Houston	206	74	489
	Jacksonville	2436	100	766
	San Diego	225	58	323
	Phoenix	1499	67	273
		Class means		
Industrial cities		2	40	106
Young cities		704	74	334
Difference		702	35	228
Significance		$p = .02$	$p < .001$	—

Sources: Column 1: same as for Table 1-2, Column 2. Column 2: same as the first source listed for Table 1-1. Column 3: same as the second source listed for Table 1-2, Column 2.

The purpose of this chapter is to relate such variations in city annexation power to the differing spatial and political endowments of the 30 large urban areas. The issue may be stated plainly. *Why should city–suburban political interaction today vary with the timing of an urban area's economic development?*

THE ROLE OF STATE POLICY GUIDELINES

Any answer to this question must take account of large-scale annexation's two broad prerequisites: "the availability of a liberal annexation law and the existence of sizable and adjacent unincorporated territory."[3] In other words, state laws must make annexation politically possible, and the central city must also remain free from complete encirclement by suburban municipalities.

Many people seem to regard encirclement as both a natural phase in any major city's spatial development and the preeminent obstacle to a city's unchecked territorial expansion. But a case can be made that the encirclement factor is itself reponsive to the character of statewide policies, and, in particular, to state laws on municipal incorporation.

So our inquiry will focus on differences in statewide annexation policies. Specifically, variations in state annexation laws will be related to the class and ethnic character of the migrants spurring a state's urban growth during its formative industrial development. The key idea here is that city borders serve not only the formal purpose of fiscal organization, but also the informal (and at times more important) function of spatially regulating social access by class and race.[4]

Demography (New York: The Free Press, 1965), chapters 6, 7, 11, and 13. An invaluable and detailed account of annexation and consolidation before 1920 is Paul Studenski, *The Government of Metropolitan Areas in the United States* (New York: National Municipal League, 1930).

2. As Table 4-1 shows, the limiting cases in 1970 were the newly consolidated city-counties of Nashville–Davidson and Jacksonville–Duval, each of which included 100% of the urbanized-area population.

3. John C. Bollens, "Metropolitan and Fringe Area Developments in 1960," *The Municipal Yearbook: 1960* (Chicago: International City Management Association, 1961), p. 58.

4. See M. N. Danielson, "Differentiation, Segregation, and Political Fragmentation in the American Metropolis," in *Governance and Population*, ed. A. E. Keir Nash (Washington, D.C.: U.S. Government Printing Office, 1972), pp. 143–176; and Oliver P. Williams, *Metropolitan Political Analysis: A Social Access Approach* (New York: Free Press, 1971), chapters 1–4.

Raymond Vernon has provided a convenient reference to this historical complementarity of the fiscal and regulatory functions of the old city's borders. He describes invasion of middle-income suburbs by the central city's poor as "a possibility to be avoided, not only for social reasons but for fiscal reasons as well. Accordingly, the zoning laws and building ordinances were quickly developed to block off the possibility.... This is warfare, not planning."[5] This chapter's guiding hypothesis is that the intensity of such "warfare" has varied greatly between the cities of the Manufacturing Belt, on the one hand, and the cities of the nation's industrial periphery, on the other.

HOUSING ENDOWMENTS AND CITY–SUBURBAN INCOME DISPARITIES

As was just mentioned, many regard the encirclement of a central city by suburban municipalities as both natural and inevitable. Buttressing this view is an image of metropolitan spatial structure that posits an abundant supply of old housing in the densely settled core, housing that will act as a magnet for the urban area's poverty population. Thus the stereotype of urban spatial structure implies the concentration of the urban poor within the central city's legal boundaries.

The one-word summary for such a spatial relationship, of course, is *filtering.* Writing in 1959 of "the cycle so far evident in the old cities," Vernon summarized filtering's spatial momentum over time as follows:

> When middle income structures reach an advanced stage of obsolescence, they will be converted to intensive low-income use. The ancient slums will be partially abandoned, as they have been in the past, for the newer ones; populations will thin out in the former and rise in the

5. Raymond Vernon, *The Myth and Reality of Our Urban Problems* (Cambridge: Harvard University Press, 1962), as excerpted in *Internal Structure of the City,* ed. Larry S. Bourne (New York: Oxford University Press, 1971), p. 19. It is instructive that Charles M. Tiebout, the seminal theorist on the economic efficiency of small-scale decentralized local government, regarded exclusionary suburban zoning as a pillar of his conceptual system: "... proper zoning laws, implicit agreements among realtors, and the like are sufficient to keep the population stable." See Tiebout, "A Pure Theory of Local Expenditures," *Journal of Political Economy,* 64 (October 1956), pp. 416–424, as reprinted in *Readings in Urban Economics,* eds. Matthew Edel and Jerome Rothenberg (New York: Macmillan, 1972), p. 518.

latter, in a wave which moves gradually outward to the edges of the city and into the older portions of the suburban towns.[6]

Any such core-to-periphery wave of obsolescence would be virtually certain to ossify formal city–suburban political lines, since it would deepen social and economic cleavages between the central city and the rest of the urban area. By this reasoning, encirclement of the central city through defensive municipal incorporations at the city's edge would indeed seem natural and inevitable.

But this scenario contains two critical logical flaws. First, although Vernon himself relates the filtering sequence explicitly to "the old cities," that essential qualification is more often forgotten. The reason the qualification matters is that filtering ought to play a far smaller role in the younger, more dispersed metropolis. To the extent that it does, then younger areas should display "softer" city–suburban political demarcations. So on this count, filtering's political impact should be limited, for the most part, to the industrial metropolis.

Second, and even more important, to grant housing endowments a contemporary political role is by no means to say that they are the ultimate historical causes of the industrial city's frozen borders. With time in mind, it may make more sense to treat housing endowments as reinforcing the already differing political endowments of industrial and younger urban areas.

To assess these issues, and to lay a groundwork for the rest of the chapter, this section relates contemporary differences in housing endowments to the timing of urban development. The historical sketch that follows treats population density and housing age (two general indicators of spatial structure) as functions of the transportation technology available during an urban area's most rapid large-scale growth. Some fairly striking empirical symmetries suggest that the distinctive legacy of turn-of-the-century development is indeed a spatial endowment reinforcing the industrial city's political isolation.

URBAN GROWTH AND RESIDENTIAL DENSITIES BEFORE 1920

Today's "industrial" cities spearheaded the nation's nineteenth-century industrialization—and manufacturing sparked the phenom-

---

6. Raymond Vernon, *The Changing Economic Function of the Central City* (New York: Committee for Economic Development, 1959), p. 66.

enal growth of these cities between the end of the Civil War and the beginning of World War I.[7] In only the first three decades after 1860, the number of manufacturing jobs in 10 of today's old cities jumped from 272,000 to 1.4 million.[8] These same cities registered the nation's largest absolute gains in population during the period; and, by 1910, they would reach about half their eventual peak sizes. (In aggregate terms, their combined populations rose from 2.6 to 12.4 million between 1860 and 1910, compared with a long-run maximum of 20.4 million in 1950.)

During all but the closing decades of this whirlwind growth, effective work-trip radii within cities hardly exceeded an hour's walking distance.[9] The signal feature of this growth as regards residential settlement was its clustering around industrial concentrations near waterfronts or railheads.[10] In other words, relative to the extensive spatial differentiation of the twentieth-century metropolis, the spatial form of these nineteenth-century industrial centers had changed little from that of the classical English factory towns.

Horse-drawn railcars had been in operation since the 1850s, but street congestion typically restricted their speed even below the maximum average of perhaps 6 miles an hour. Although railroads had facilitated the rise of primordial commuting villages as early as the 1850s, railroads and cable cars exerted only a minimal influence on intraurban settlement patterns. It was only after 1890—a year in which 70% of city trackage was still committed to horse-drawn cars—

7. A standard source on the role of manufacturing in the creation of the American urban network after the Civil War is Eric E. Lampard, "The Evolving System of Cities in the United States: Urbanization and Economic Development," in *Issues in Urban Economics,* eds. Harvey S. Perloff and Lowdon Wingo, Jr. (Baltimore: Johns Hopkins Press, 1968), pp. 81–139.

8. The comparison refers to Baltimore, Boston, Chicago, Cleveland, Detroit, New York, Philadelphia, Pittsburgh, San Francisco, and St. Louis. Figures for the individual cities appear in a table (the source for the totals in the text) in Alan R. Pred, *The Spatial Dynamics of U.S. Urban-Industrial Growth,* 1800–1914 (Cambridge: MIT Press, 1966), p. 20.

9. This and the following paragraphs draw heavily on Charles N. Glaab and Theodore A. Brown, *A History of Urban America* (New York: Macmillan, 1967), pp. 147–154; and also on Sam Bass Warner, Jr., *Streetcar Suburbs: The Process of Growth in Boston, 1870–1900,* paperback edition (New York: Atheneum, 1970), pp. 15–25. Warner (p. 22) notes that horsecar service in Boston had by 1887 brought "the outer edge of good transportation to four miles from City Hall," that is, from the city center.

10. David Ward, *Cities and Immigrants: A Geography of Change in Nineteenth-Century America* (New York: Oxford University Press, 1971), chapter 3.

that widespread adoption of electrified trolley and subway systems really broke the tie that bound residential settlements to industrial sites. When the conversion came, it came quickly: 97% of city trackage had been electrified by 1902. But by this time, much of the new population had already been housed in accordance with pre-electrical modes of transit.[11]

The relation between this sequence and residential densities—and also the impact of still-to-come urban highway systems—was spelled out by a gifted turn-of-the-century observer.

> When a pair of legs was the only vehicle of locomotion the ordinary man could afford, large cities were unavoidably compressed into small quarters. The horsecar and the [horse-drawn] bus added perhaps a mile or two to this area, but did not dispense with the necessity of severely economizing space. The trolley has stretched it out several miles further, while future improvement in the machinery of transit may well make any spot within 50 miles of the center of an important city available as a place of residence for its wage earners.[12]

It need hardly be stressed that the internal combustion engine, harnessed in the truck and the automobile, would bring just such a "future improvement," one making 50-mile commuting radii an eventual reality.

THE PERSISTENCE OF URBAN SPATIAL DIFFERENCES

The broad implications for settlement patterns seem clear enough. Quantum changes in the technology of urban transit imply not only a layering of incrementally lower-density rings in the industrial metropolis, but also sharply lower aggregate densities in entire urban areas, the main growth of which would come after 1920—in the auto age. In short, the history of urban transportation technology leads us to expect clear contrasts in the average densities of, say, Phoenix, on the one hand, and an ancient industrial metropolis of similar size, like Buffalo, on the other. Furthermore, because housing lasts so long, we might also expect related differences in the arrangement and age of the housing stocks of the two areas.

The logic of such spatial contrasts could easily be recast in theoretical terms, that is, in the language of transportation costs, land rents,

11. Glaab and Brown, *Urban America*, pp. 154–159.
12. Quoted, but not identified, in Glaab and Brown, *Urban America*, p. 154.

and residential densities. A complete translation is hardly necessary here. But a little theory can go a long way to show why initially differing spatial regimes should persist even after the dictates of transportation technology have been completely altered.

The key theoretical point, illuminated in two essays by Harrison and Kain, is at once simple and powerful.[13] When a city develops in a "compressed" pattern, that initial concentration of residents creates high land rents. In turn, high rents encourage *continued* intensive use of capital with land, that is, continued high-density development of central sites.

The Harrison and Kain essays dealt with this reciprocal relationship between initial densities and location rents in 83 metropolitan areas over a 90-year period. They observed that "during each time period, the density of urban development is strongly influenced by the level of location rents prevailing in each metropolitan area."[14] Meantime, what determined the level of location rents was "the number of households competing for residential sites" (i.e., *existing* densities). They went on to report a model of layered, incremental densities, which when tested found areawide densities varying clearly with the timing of urban development.

In sum, both the brute facts of transportation history and the refinements of economic theory would lead us to expect long-lived contrasts in residential settlement patterns. The evidence is not at odds with such expectations. Table 4-2 shows that densities and housing age diverge sharply between younger and older urban areas, and even more decisively between their central cities. In brief,

1. Using round numbers, the dozen industrial areas had average densities of 4500 persons per square mile in 1970, or almost twice the younger-area average of 2700.

2. The share of the industrial area's 1970 housing stock built before 1939 averaged 49%, compared with only 22% in the younger areas.

3. Because the young city's borders cover larger shares of the urban-area population and thus include more new peripheral de-

---

13. David Harrison, Jr. and John F. Kain, "An Historical Model of Urban Form," Harvard University Program on Regional and Urban Economics, Discussion Paper No. 63; and "Cumulative Urban Growth and Urban Density Functions," *Journal of Urban Economics*, 1 (January 1974), pp. 61–98.

14. Harrison and Kain, "Urban Form," pp. 44–45.

TABLE 4-2
Structural Contrasts among Urbanized Areas of Differing Ages, 1970

Age class	Urbanized area	Population density per square mile (thousands)	Percentage of housing stock built before 1939
Industrial	New York	6.7	53
	Chicago	5.3	49
	Philadelphia	5.3	53
	Boston	4.0	65
	Pittsburgh	3.1	55
	St. Louis	4.1	44
	San Francisco	4.4	38
	Baltimore	5.1	42
	Cleveland	3.0	46
	Buffalo	5.1	58
	Detroit	4.6	38
	Cincinnati	3.3	48
Anomalous	Los Angeles	5.3	23
	Washington	5.0	22
	Milwaukee	2.7	46
	Kansas City	2.2	38
	New Orleans	5.2	36
	Seattle	3.0	30
Young	Indianapolis	2.2	37
	Atlanta	2.7	18
	Denver	3.6	27
	Columbus	3.4	32
	Memphis	3.4	22
	Nashville	1.3	24
	Dallas	2.0	15
	San Antonio	3.5	24
	Houston	3.1	15
	Jacksonville	1.5	21
	San Diego	3.1	17
	Phoenix	2.2	9
Means and significance of mean differences			
Industrial cities		4.5	49
Young cities		2.7	22
Difference		1.8	27
Significance		$p < .001$	$p < .001$

Sources: Column 1: same as the first source for Table 1-1. Column 2: U.S. Bureau of the Census, *1970 Census of Housing: Housing Characteristics for States, Cities, and Counties.*

velopment, *central-city* contrasts are doubly striking (see Table 4-3). Here, average density differs not by 2000 but by fully 10,000 persons per square mile. And now the pre-1939 housing share differs not by 27 but by nearly 43 percentage points.

FILTERING AND CITY – SUBURBAN INCOME DISPARITIES

If spatial endowments differ so much between industrial and post-industrial urban area, the spatial impact of filtering would seem to be mainly an older-area phenomenon. As a test of this notion, we might consider the final step in the filtering sequence—the concentration of the poor in old core housing. By the terms of the argument, contrasts in housing endowments should be matched by like differences in the spatial distribution of the rich and the poor. And so they are.

As we saw in Chapter 3, average family incomes in most young central cities equaled or exceeded those of suburban families in 1970. The pattern is neither uniform nor very pronounced in itself, but it takes on a certain clarity when compared with the older area's severe income disparities. In the industrial metropolis, of course, average incomes of city families fall consistently below those of their suburban counterparts. By contrast, the younger area's more recent development has created a different housing endowment and a surprisingly undifferentiated scatter of incomes between central city and fringe.

Thus the first qualification to the conventional assumptions about filtering and city–suburban political divisions is very much in order. The facts warn against assuming any broad applicability of the stereotype of old, dense core housing.

But that still leaves the second problem of interpretation: whether the industrial city's massive supply of dense and deteriorated housing is the historical *cause* of the city's political isolation. We have established beyond a reasonable doubt that the older area's housing stock at least intensifies city–suburban political cleavages today. To say whether it created such cleavages in the first place, we need more information about the end of the industrial city's territorial expansion. If, for example, the old city's borders were frozen a half-century or more ago, then contemporary housing endowments could hardly qualify as the explanation. Instead, both spatial and political endowments would represent separate (independent) byproducts of the industrial area's development.

TABLE 4-3

Structural Contrasts among Central Cities of Differing Ages, 1970

Age class	City, by 1910 metropolitan size	Population density per square mile (thousands)	Percentage of housing stock built before 1939	Average household income: city–SMSA ring ratio
Industrial	New York	26.3	62	66
	Chicago	15.1	67	73
	Philadelphia	15.2	69	75
	Boston	13.9	77	69
	Pittsburgh	9.4	74	89
	St. Louis	10.2	74	70
	San Francisco	15.8	67	81
	Baltimore	11.6	60	65
	Cleveland	9.9	73	65
	Buffalo	11.2	86	105
	Detroit	11.0	62	82
	Cincinnati	5.8	59	85
Anomalous	Los Angeles	6.1	32	92
	Washington	12.4	47	95
	Milwaukee	7.6	55	73
	Kansas City	1.6	51	81
	New Orleans	3.0	50	86
	Seattle	6.4	48	81
Young	Indianapolis	1.9	40	107
	Atlanta	3.8	30	89
	Denver	5.4	41	89
	Columbus	4.0	39	118
	Memphis	2.9	23	104
	Nashville	0.8	25	129
	Dallas	3.2	18	102
	San Antonio	3.6	26	70
	Houston	2.8	17	104
	Jacksonville	0.7	21	—
	San Diego	2.2	22	98
	Phoenix	2.3	11	103
Means and significance of mean differences				
Industrial cities		13.0	69	77
Young cities		2.8	26	101
Difference		10.2	43	24
Significance		$p < .001$	$p < .001$	$p < .001$

Sources: Column 1: same as the first source for Table 1-1. Column 2: same as for Table 4-2, Column 2. Column 3: same as for Table 3-5, Column 3.

The issue, then, is just when the industrial city's territorial expansion came to an end.

THE TERRITORIAL HISTORIES OF
YOUNG AND OLD CITIES

If the large-scale filtering of the housing stock is an historically recent phase in American urban development, whatever sealing of city borders occurred before that phase must have other sources. The point of this section is that all the industrial cities did in fact lose their annexation power long ago.

THE ERA OF INDUSTRIAL-CITY ANNEXATIONS: 1850 – 1930

A theme of the chapter is that today's differences in central-city annexation power reflect underlying differences in the broad developmental experiences of young and old urban areas. A standard urban geography textbook yields a tantalizing suggestion in this regard:

> Until about 1900, American cities added land by annexation with no particular difficulty. Beginning at approximately that time, however, people's attitudes toward annexation began to change, and many states adopted provisions that made annexation more difficult. Annexations became less frequent and were mostly limited to small, unincorporated areas just outside the city's borders.[15]

Judging by the historical evidence, Murphy's account applies not to "American cities" generally, but rather to the specific cities that were large at the turn of the century. Thus delimited, the passage offers a good introduction to the territorial histories of the industrial cities.

Annexation data reported in R. D. McKenzie's classic, *The Metropolitan Community*, provide territorial records for the industrial cities going back to the middle of the last century.[16] His evidence is summarized in Figure 4-1, which portrays the land area added by the 30 cities as a group for each decade of the century between 1850 and

15. Raymond E. Murphy, *The American City: An Urban Geography* (New York: McGraw-Hill, 1966), p. 421.
16. New York: McGraw-Hill, 1933, appendix table 1.

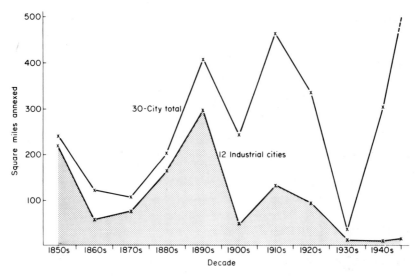

Figure 4-1. Territory annexed by the 30 largest cities: 1850 – 1950.

1950. The territory added by the industrial cities as a class is shown in the shaded area.

The figure shows vigorous territorial expansion by the old-city class until the first decade of the century. Some of the 12 cities evidently continued to annex through the 1920s, although by that time, their share of the total had fallen precipitously from the late nineteenth century. Then, after 1930, their collective territorial history virtually ended.

So, by this reading, the watershed was less the turn of the century than the Great Depression. Nor should the 1930s seem an unexpected break-point. For cities generally, the Depression created a moratorium on urban growth. As peripheral development dried up, annexation activity abruptly ceased. The economic stimulus from World War II rekindled urban growth across the nation, and, by the late 1940s, large-scale annexations also resumed. But the post-1945 annexation resurgence was selective: It excluded the old cities.

In short, an initial overview of the evidence suggests two possible revisions in Murphy's argument that turn-of-the-century changes in state laws ended large-scale annexations. For one thing, whatever changes were made constrained only the industrial cities. Second, such constraints apparently took hold at different times in different old cities, acquiring full force only after 1930.

Such generalizations should, of course, be checked against the records of individual cities. To that end, Figure 4-2 presents graphical comparisons of the number of square miles *each city* added during two periods, 1850–1930 and 1930–1970. The results prove highly consistent: Widespread and substantial increases on the part of the industrial cities marked the first period, just as the young cities' annexations dominated the second.

The figure discloses that the young cities have not simply replicated the territorial expansions of today's old cities. Not only the timing, but also the sheer scale of annexation has varied by age-class. As can be verified in Table 4-4, today most young cities cover considerably larger land areas than cities whose borders froze early. Here, then, is a second perspective on the differing fiscal environments affecting young and old cities.

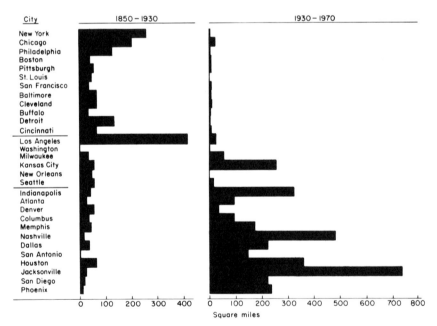

Figure 4-2. Territory added by the 30 largest cities: 1850–1930, 1930–1970.

TABLE 4-4

Land Areas of the 30 Largest Cities: 1850, 1930, 1970

	City, by 1910 metropolitan size	Land area (square miles)			Territory added	
		1970	1930	1850	1930–1970	1850–1930
Industrial	New York	300	299	[41]^a	1	258
	Chicago	223	202	10	21	201
	Philadelphia	128	128	2	0	128
	Boston	46	44	5	2	39
	Pittsburgh	55	51	2	4	51
	St. Louis	61	61	14	0	47
	San Francisco	45	42	5	3	37
	Baltimore	78	79	13	−1	66
	Cleveland	76	71	5	5	66
	Buffalo	41	39	4	2	35
	Detroit	138	138	6	0	133
	Cincinnati	78	71	6	7	66
Anomalous	Los Angeles	464	440	[29]	23	413
	Washington	61	61	60	0	0
	Milwaukee	95	42	7	54	35
	Kansas City	316	59	[4]	258	54
	New Orleans	197	196	148	1	48
	Seattle	84	68	[11]	15	57
Young	Indianapolis	379	54	[11]	325	43
	Atlanta	132	35	[9]	97	26
	Denver	95	58	[4]	37	55
	Columbus	135	38	2	96	37
	Memphis	217	46	2	172	44
	Nashville	508	26	[9]	482	16
	Dallas	266	42	[9]	224	36
	San Antonio	184	36	36	148	0
	Houston	434	72	9	362	63
	Jacksonville	766	26	1	740	25
	San Diego	317	94	74	223	20
	Phoenix	248	10	[10]	238	10

Source: Same as for Table 3-10.

^a Brackets indicate earliest known land area.

So the categorical differences in the timing and scale of annexation are unmistakable. The hypothesis is that late-nineteenth-century development somehow "necessitated" the freezing of the industrial city's borders. To assess its initial plausibility, we require a city-by-city chronology of the end of annexation.

But how should "the end" of annexation be measured? Our concern is not the last, desperate square mile a city added. On the contrary, it is the end of *large-scale* territorial expansion that is of interest. "Large-scale" is, of course, a relative concept, one having different connotations in cities with different population sizes and different absolute land areas today. So any precise operational measure must remain in part arbitrary. That much said, let us select the decade a city reached 90% of its 1970 land area as the one signaling the end of the city's large-scale territorial expansion.

Table 4-5 lists the critical decades, so derived, for each of the 30 largest cities. Here is the chronology we need for a first reading on the hypothesis. Unfortunately, however, there is no obvious pattern in the table to establish the notion of a simple one-to-one relationship between the timing of urban development and the end of central-city annexation. In particular, some half-dozen of the 30 cities stopped increasing their land areas long before the turn of the century. Indeed, the borders of Buffalo, Philadelphia, San Francisco, and Washington froze even before the Civil War! And St. Louis ceased to expand soon after, in the 1870s.

As the Washington case might suggest, however, most of these examples of early territorial crystallization can be explained in a way that does little damage to the larger argument. The explanation lies in the formal distinction—ignored until now—between annexation and city–county consolidation. Annexation involves a shift in municipal borders, a change that need not preclude further redefinitions thereafter. But when a city expands its territory by merging with or separating from its surrounding county, the change has usually created new and immutable *county* lines. In other words, just as Washington represents the special case of a "city–state," so, too, do city–counties tend to become as rigidly delineated as other counties in the national network.

The correlation between fixed borders and city–county reorganization can be seen in Table 4-6. The table gives the dates of major

TABLE 4-5
Critical Decades in the Territorial Histories of the 30 Largest Cities

Decade city's land area passed 90% of 1970 total	Cities with critical decades before 1930	Cities with critical decades after 1930
Pre-1850	Washington	
1850s	Buffalo Philadelphia San Francisco	
1870s	New Orleans St. Louis	
1890s	New York	
1910s	Baltimore Boston Cincinnati	
1920s	Chicago Cleveland Detroit Los Angeles Pittsburgh	
1950s		Atlanta Dallas Milwaukee Seattle
1960s		Columbus Denver Jacksonville Houston Indianapolis Kansas City Memphis Nashville Phoenix San Antonio San Diego

Source: Same as for Table 3-10.

TABLE 4-6
City–County Reorganizations as Checks to Further Territorial Growth

City	Year of merger or separation as a county	Resulting land area (square miles)	Subsequent territory added
(Washington)	(pre-1850)	(61)	(0)
Baltimore	1851	13	55
Philadelphia	1854	128	0
San Francisco	1856	42	0
New Orleans	1874	196	0
St. Louis	1875	61	0
New York	1898	299	0
Denver	1903	59	37
Nashville	1963	508	—
Jacksonville	1968	766	—
Indianapolis	1970	379	—

Source: John A. Rush, *The City–County Consolidated* (Los Angeles: published by the author, 1941), and Paul Studenski, *The Government of Metropolitan Areas in the United States* (New York: National Municipal League, 1930).

city–county consolidations, together with each city–county's subsequent territorial growth. By way of background, in 1970 the 30 largest cities included 10 outright city–counties; the city–state of Washington, and a functionally, although not formally consolidated system in Boston. Of the 10 formal city–counties, three have been created only during the past 15 years, whereas the other seven date back to the latter half of the nineteenth century (or, in Denver's case, to 1903).

For five of the seven long-time city–counties, reorganization created permanently fixed borders. In chronological order, Philadelphia, San Francisco, New Orleans, St. Louis, and New York all became city–counties before 1900, and none has added a square mile since. Only in Baltimore and Denver did the newly created borders remain flexible. In Baltimore, even this flexibility was temporary; by 1920, the city's borders were frozen.

So with this qualification, the chronology begins to look more consistent with the hypothesis. By way of recapitulation, it seems that the 30 different territorial histories can be described by means of two or three brief "rules":

1. A handful of the 30 central cities stopped growing territorially before 1900, consequent to a merger with (or reorganization as) a county. While the resulting city–county's ability to alter its borders was a state-by-state question, the only one which has managed to do so since 1920 is Denver, a young city.

2. In nearly all the remaining cases, a city's post-1945 annexation power has varied with the timing of its ascent to large size, that is, with whether it became large before World War I, or later.

3. The only anomalies among all 30 cities are Buffalo and Los Angeles.

This brief overview of the historical record points up the likelihood that annexation's ground rules have been made more difficult for industrial than for young cities. In some old cities, we have seen that municipal land areas were fixed "naturally," following a city–county reorganization. For the others, we might expect to find overt evidence of especially restrictive state procedures.

THE RULES OF THE GAME

The question remains to be explored. Why should city–suburban political interaction vary so starkly between cities whose economic functions derive from contrasting periods of American economic development? By Murphy's account, "people's attitudes... began to change" around the turn of the century, and states moved to abridge traditional city annexation powers. To judge from the record of city territorial expansion, something of this sort may very well have curtailed annexation by the industrial cities. But whatever did happen had little or no impact on young cities. And the account raises other questions as well.

1. Whose attitudes changed, and why?
2. How were changes in the climate of opinion translated into changes in policy?
3. Is there a demonstrable legacy today of especially restrictive ground rules in the states containing old cities?

My answers to these questions are based on an essay by M. N. Danielson—one implication of which is that statewide annexation policies should indeed differ systematically between the Manufacturing Belt and the rest of the nation.[17] In this section, I will develop and test a formal hypothesis to that effect. In essence, the hypothesis is that *state annexation laws differ because the social uses of American cities differ*—in line with the timing of their industrial development.

EXIT, VOICE, AND LOYALTY IN THE TURN-OF-THE-CENTURY CITY

The relatively sudden industrialization of the American economy after the Civil War permanently changed the political character of the nation's then larger cities. Historians describe the preindustrial (or mercantile) city as a workable community, in which people of varying occupations and social ranks lived and worked in close proximity, with only routine social friction.[18] But industrialization, fueled by the massive influx of non-English-speaking workers, brought newly pronounced class distinctions to the growing industrial centers. In short, the context for the transportation breakthroughs described earlier was a socially divided industrial city. Thus it is not surprising that the first wave of large-scale urban decentralization after 1890 gave vent to the spatial articulation of class and ethnic conflict.

During the height of the urban–industrial transformation, between 1880 and 1920, in a mass migration without parallel in world history, more than 23 million people immigrated to the United States.[19] After 1896, a growing majority of the new arrivals were so-called New Immigrants—a term used at the time to distinguish Italians, Slavs, and Eastern European Jews from their more easily assimilated predecessors from the British Isles, Scandinavia, and Germany. The New Immigrants fled ravaged rural areas of Southern and Eastern Europe in search of jobs in an American economy that, at least in times of expansion, had an almost unlimited demand for unskilled labor. Once in this country, therefore, their destinations were governed primarily by the location of industrial activity. Thus, between 1900 and 1909, alone, roughly *5 million* New Immigrants moved into the booming cities of the Manufacturing Belt.[20]

17. See Note 4, page 65.
18. See Glaab and Brown, *Urban America*, p. 84, and Sam Bass Warner, Jr., *The Private City: Philadelphia in Three Periods of Its Growth*, paperback edition (Philadelphia: University of Pennsylvania Press, 1971), p. 50.
19. Ward, *Cities and Immigrants*, p. 53.
20. *Ibid.*, pp. 53–57.

By 1910, immigrants and their children constituted absolute majorities within the industrial cities. For all cities of 100,000 or more, the 1910 census found the average proportion of "foreign-stock" (i.e., foreign-born and the children of foreign-born parents) residents to be fully 58%.[21] In the cities of the Manufacturing Belt (and 34 of the 50 cities above 100,000 in 1910 were in the Manufacturing Belt), the foreign-stock share often exceeded two-thirds.[22]

Although such numbers suggest something about the enormous social impact immigration had on the nation's large cities, they greatly exaggerate the New Immigrants' political influence. "Although the foreign stock were the majority in urban areas, *their function was typically to fill the manual occupations necessary for industrial growth.*"[23] To this extent, the industrial cities' immigrant populations resembled the urban proletariats of Europe: numerically impressive, but concentrated at the lower rungs of the social and economic ladder. Moreover, and unlike European workers, urban immigrants in this country were ethnically fractionated—set off into mutually suspicious camps, and thus doubly isolated.

As has become legend, such political power as the New Immigrants enjoyed was earned with the votes they could deliver to the boss-ruled political machines then running most large cities.[24] Ameliorative social services from the federal government were unheard of before the New Deal. Nor did private charity or state government services— each of which did, however, become increasingly important after 1900—make much difference to most immigrants. By contrast, the big-city political machines rewarded entire blocs of foreign-stock voters with ritualistic and substantive political services.

So much is standard textbook history. Less clearly defined is the response urban native-stock whites made to the immigrant–machine alliances.[25]

21. *Ibid.*, p. 52.

22. *Ibid.*, p. 51.

23. Lance E. Davis *et al.*, *American Economic Growth: An Economist's History of the United States* (New York: Harper & Row, 1972), p. 138. (Emphasis added.)

24. Robert K. Merton, *Social Theory and Social Structure* (New York: The Free Press, 1957), pp. 71–82, reprinted as "Latent Functions of the Machine," in *American Urban History,* ed. Alexander B. Callow, Jr. (New York: Oxford University Press, 1973), pp. 220–229.

25. An excellent treatment of the nativist response to the New Immigration is John Higham, *Strangers in the Land: Patterns of Nativism, 1860–1925* (New Brunswick, New Jersey: Rutgers University Press, 1955).

A veritable library of popular and scholarly works alike describes the Progressive response to what Lincoln Steffans called *The Shame of the Cities*—the corruption of city governments by political machines— in his book of 1904. The traditional literature documents the attempts of Progressive reformers to attain their due voice in the affairs of city government, in part through appeals to higher governments for structural reforms.[26] In the terms Albert O. Hirschman has introduced, the urban Progressives' attempts to gain *voice* evidenced their continuing *loyalty* to the city, and to the idea of honest and efficient city government.[27]

More recent studies suggest, however, that at least as important in the long view was the *exit* option technology afforded large numbers of middle-class, native-stock whites.[28] The electric streetcar and, later, the automobile offered purely technical solutions to the extreme urban crowding of the day. But they also provided political "solutions" to the alien environment of the boss-dominated, immigrant-swollen city. In giving the emerging middle class the power to put greater distance between their homes and their jobs, the new technologies allowed them to exit the inner areas of the city for the periphery. In this sense the Progressive quest for greater voice may have mattered less in real terms than the middle class's option simply to renounce its political affiliation by moving beyond the city's borders.

In sum, the decades bracketing 1900 gave rise not just to a decentralized metropolis, but to an urban landscape in which core and periphery were increasingly differentiated by class and national origin. Technological innovations had fundamentally altered the terms of the urban political game—the contest for spatial control of social access.[29]

In an essay on this turn-of-the-century rehearsal for contemporary white flight, an urban historian goes to the heart of the matter:

> In reviewing this material, it is difficult not to conclude that many who advocated decentralization were as motivated by considerations of social control as by a desire to enable men to live more comfortable or

26. Norman I. Fainstein and Susan S. Fainstein, *Urban Political Movements: The Search for Power by Minority Groups in American Cities* (Englewood Cliffs, New Jersey: Prentice-Hall, 1974), pp. 14–30.

27. Albert O. Hirschman, *Exit, Voice, and Loyalty: Responses to Decline in Firms, Organizations, and States* (Cambridge: Harvard University Press, 1970).

28. Ward, *Cities and Immigrants* chapter 5; and M. H. Yeates and B. J. Garner, *The North American City* (New York: Harper & Row, 1971), chapter 8.

29. Williams, *Metropolitan Political Analysis*, chapters 1–4.

healthy lives. . . . Transit systems, by making it possible for working people to leave the unhealthy city for arcadian suburbs, offered a relatively inexpensive method for curtailing the threat of the slum.[30]

EXIT, ANNEXATION, AND CONTAINMENT

Annexation represented an obviously critical variable in this early spatial polarization of the industrial metropolis. In stylized outline, the core of the metropolis had three functional components.[31] Around a port or railhead were the factories—at once the wellspring and the focal point of the city's growth. Industrial workers, unable to afford either better housing or the transportation expense to reach it, lived in ethnically distinct neighborhoods, or quarters, in the nearby tenement zone. Immediately adjacent to the industrial area was a flourishing central business district, which, in some cities, provided as many jobs as the industrial zone itself.

Although dependent on the central business district for jobs, the native-stock middle-class could partially escape the environment of the immigrant tenements by moving to new residential districts at the city's periphery. But so long as the city government retained its annexation power, there remained no escape from the political dominion of the machine. As Danielson writes, the interaction of spatial differentiation and the political presence of the machine "structured political conflict in the industrial city along class-based territorial lines."[32] Such de facto lines would engender de jure local boundaries only if the city's annexation power could be neutralized.

Thus the background to Danielson's explanation of the end of the industrial city's annexation power:

the underlying cause for the end of annexation and the political containment of the city was the almost universal desire of the periphery for political autonomy from the core. . . . Success crowned the annexation efforts of the outer areas because most state governments were sympathetic to the suburban communities and hostile to the cities and their ruling political factions.[33]

30. Joel Arthur Tarr, "From City to Suburb: The 'Moral' Influence of Transportation Technology," in *American Urban History,* ed. Alexander B. Callow (New York: Oxford University Press, 1973), pp. 202–212.

31. Ward, *Cities and Immigrants,* chapter 3.

32. Danielson, "Differentiation, Segregation, and Political Fragmentation," p. 149.

33. *Ibid.,* pp. 149–150.

In response to petitions by residents of outlying areas, he continues, state governments began to redefine the basic ground rules of local fiscal organization:

1. To circumvent the periphery's dependence on city utilities, some states mandated the extension of city services beyond the city's borders.

2. To accomplish the same end others fostered independent special-service districts.

3. To give outlying areas a veto over the city's annexations, "double-majority" statutes were introduced, whereby annexations had to be approved by majority votes in both the city *and* the area to be annexed.[34]

4. Finally, municipal incorporation laws were eased so that peripheral areas could stake out inviolate boundaries of their own.[35]

As an aside, it is in the context that suburban encirclement may be seen as responsive to statewide annexation policy. Encirclement depends on easy incorporation laws. As an authority on the question wrote years ago: "The process of surrounding a city with a multitude of small incorporated places has been adopted deliberately in many states to prevent annexation except by vote of the people to be annexed."[36] In this light, encirclement looks natural and inevitable only as a natural expression of core–periphery conflict in the turn-of-the-century metropolis.

So we have a clearly defined, refutable hypothesis. The upshot of the industrial city's turn-of-the-century polarization should be a legacy of unusually restrictive annexation laws in the states of the Manufacturing Belt today. Putting it differently, the proposition is that central-city borders in the industrial metropolis perform the latent function of "containing" the urban poor, a function state governments sanctioned half a century and more ago.

ANNEXATION LAWS IN THE ECONOMY'S CORE AND PERIPHERY

The converse is that the states *outside* the Manufacturing Belt should have markedly easier annexation guidelines. By reason of both

34. John C. Bollens and Henry J. Schmandt, *The Metropolis,* second edition (New York: Harper & Row, 1970), pp. 283–285.

35. Danielson, "Differentiation, Segregation, and Political Fragmentation," p. 150.

36. Thomas H. Reed, "Progress in Metropolitan Integration," *Public Administration Review,* 9 (Winter 1949), p. 5.

timing and geography, city–suburban conflict in the younger metropolis has been comparatively mild. In the first place, younger urban areas have developed under a technological regime encouraging both decentralized industrial production and dispersed, low-density housing. Equally important, their "city-building" phase has been based largely on the influx of native-stock whites from the declining rural areas of the South and the Midwest.[37]

The contrasting origins of the younger area's migrant population deserve emphasis. Most younger areas (Columbus and Indianapolis excepted) lie outside the Manufacturing Belt, at great distances from the major eastern ports of entry. For this reason, and because their main development came only after World War I, the then smaller cities received few New Immigrants. In 1910, for example, at the crescendo of the New Immigration, only *one out of six* of the foreign-born lived outside the Manufacturing Belt.[38] World War I drastically reduced the immigrant wave, and, in 1924, free imigration's myriad opponents finally prevailed upon Congress and the president to enact a law with strict national-origin quotas.[39] In short, younger urban areas experienced large-scale growth only after the New Immigration had been shut off.

The hallmarks of postindustrial urban development have been incisively defined by T. R. Fehrenbach, a Texas historian. In his words, "Texas did not industrialize in the pattern of the northern or midwestern states. This led to striking though not always apparent divergences." In particular,

> Urbanization came very late to Texas.... The cities grew up and outward in the automobile age, primarily as merchantile, financial, and distribution centers, without much industrialization.... And as the state became almost 80 percent urban, the cities were peopled primarily from the surrounding countryside, by the families who fled or were forced from the teeming agrarian counties, two-thirds of which lost population steadily in this century.[40]

As a result of their shared backgrounds and values, the rural migrants of the Southwest posed no particular threat to the established

37. See Roy Lubove, "The Urbanization Process," *Journal of the American Institute of Planners,* 33 (January 1967), pp. 33–39, reprinted in *American Urban History,* ed. Alexander B. Callow, Jr. (New York: Oxford University Press, 1973), p. 661.

38. Ward, *Cities and Immigrants,* p. 60.

39. Davis *et al., American Economic Growth,* p. 126.

40. T. R. Fehrenbach, "Seven Keys to Understanding Texas," *The Atlantic Monthly,* March 1975, p. 124.

elites of Texas's growing urban centers. "Urbanization occurred without the large-scale industrialization of other parts of America, and consequently the organizational forms and attitudes of the industrial society of the North were slow to appear." Above all, Texas cities escaped the demographic and political clashes that had polarized the industrial metropolis:

> Here arose a subtle but very real difference between the society of Texas and of the other great states. . . . In most Texas communities, large or small, economic, social, and political power did not fragment as in the complex, ethnically mixed northern metropolises. All were held and exercised by the same people, as they were everywhere in eighteenth-century [i.e., preindustrial] America.[41]

It happens that Texas has one of the nation's most permissive annexation laws. Under the terms of our hypothesis, that is by no means a coincidence. Instead, Texas's easy law is viewed as a reflection of the relative ethnic and social homogeneity of Texas's urban population. The task now is to generalize the hypothesis so as to put it to a formal test.

The Ground Rules for Young and Old Cities

A prerequisite to comparing the difficulty of state annexation laws, of course, is a discriminating and consistent rating scale. At one end of the scale we might place states whose cities can annex new territory more or less at will. At the other end would lie states in which only state legislature may preside over central-city annexations. Between these two extremes, some provision should be made for the voting procedures used in areas to be annexed by the city. In other words, such a scale should reflect the several variables in the process: who initiates the action, the vote required for a veto by outlying residents, and the state legislature's powers of intervention.

An index with just this sort of precision has already been devised by Raymond Wheeler.[42] He used three criteria to assign state-laws scores ranging from 0 to 5. If only suburban residents could initiate annexation, for example, the state law was rated 1; if the city government

---

41. *Ibid.*, p. 125.

42. Raymond H. Wheeler, "Annexation Law and Annexation Success," *Land Economics,* 41 (November 1965), pp. 354–360.

could initiate the process, the score assigned was 0. On the other two criteria—the method of confirmation and the method of approval in the area to be annexed—scores ranged from 0 to 2. Then each state law received the sum of the three component scores as its rating. So the "easiest" laws had scores of 0, the hardest, 5.

Wheeler's rating system permits us to compare the laws affecting young and old cities. Of the 21 states containing one or more of the 30 largest cities in 1970, 13 had only young or only old cities within their borders. (In other words, the other 8 states contained anomalous cities or cities from two or three different age categories; examples are California, Missouri, and Ohio.) By the simplest reading of our argument, the states containing only industrial cities should have more restrictive laws than those containing only young cities.

This first comparison is depicted in Table 4-7, which ranks the 13 states according to their scores on the 0–5 scale. The table makes one point very clear: All six of the states containing only industrial cities had relatively restrictive laws. All six, in other words, scored 3 or higher on the scale. This is the expected result. It suggests that an ultimate cause for the industrial city's territorial isolation is deliberate state policy.

At the same time, however, not all the states containing only young cities had easy annexation laws. The fact that all the young cities did manage large-scale annexations anyway is very much in line with Wheeler's findings. His purpose was to relate the incidence of successful annexations to the ease of difficulty of formal procedures; hence the scale. While he did find a clear correlation between annexation law and annexation success, its strength varied with the age and the region of the cities considered. In essence, he found that younger cities in the South and West were less constrained by restrictive state laws than older cities of the East and Midwest.[43] In short, the pattern of Table 4-7 discloses an additional point of interest. Not only are the laws affecting old cities generally more restrictive, but a restrictive law seems to generate a greater impact on old cities than on young ones.

Annexation Laws in the Manufacturing Belt and the South

Now we can formally test the underlying regional pattern of variation—and its congruence with pre-World War I industrial

43. *Ibid.*, p. 357.

TABLE 4-7
Annexation Laws Affecting Young and Old Cities

Restrictiveness of annexation law, by Wheeler's rating		States containing young cities	States containing old cities
("Easy")	0	Indiana Tennessee Texas	
	1		
	2	Arizona	
	3	Colorado Florida	Illinois Michigan Pennsylvania
	4		
("Hard")	5	Georgia	Massachusetts Maryland New York

development. Under the terms of the hypothesis, we expect the states of the old industrial core, the Manufacturing Belt, to have especially restrictive laws. The 12 states I will select for the test are those contained in the area whose four corners are Boston, Baltimore, St. Louis, and Milwaukee.[44] These 12 states, the destinations of the overwhelming majority of New Immigrants, contain 10 of the 12 industrial cities.

By the same token, we expect to find the easiest laws today in states least affected by heavy industrialization and the New Immigration. The states that were least industrialized (and least urbanized) at the turn of the century were, of course, in the South. For a precise enumeration, we may adopt the regional definitions Perloff and his associates used to compare historical variations in regional levels of urbanization and industrialization.[45] The resulting list includes all the states of the Southern Rim except California, as well as such border states as Kentucky, Virginia, and West Virginia. The 16 states so selected contain 8 of the 12 young cities.

44. Missouri, part of which constitutes the western edge of the Manufacturing Belt, is omitted from the list because the state's annexation law differs as between St. Louis and other Missouri cities.

45. Harvey S. Perloff et al., Regions, Resources, and Economic Growth (Baltimore: Johns Hopkins Press, 1960), pp. 5–7.

These are the two broad regional groupings employed in Table 4-8. It may be seen by inspection that the table supports the contention that annexation laws are sharply more restrictive in the Manufacturing Belt than in the South. The clarity of the contrast is unmistakable. Eight of the southern (versus only one of the industrial) states had laws rated at 0 or 1. At the other end of the scale, six of the seven states with "hard" laws (i.e., rated at 4 or 5) were in the Manufacturing Belt.

The contrast can be summarized via the mean scores for each region. For the 16 southern states, the average score is 1.4, as compared with 3.6 for the 12 industrial states. In other words, if we thought of the states as lying somewhere on a 100-point scale, the southern-state average would be 28, or well under half the industrial state average of 72. A standard nonparametric test (the Wilcoxon rank-sum test) indicates that this difference is statistically significant at a probability value of .001.[46] So, to the extent that Wheeler's scale is a reliable yardstick, we can say that *annexation laws are well over twice as restrictive in the old industrial core as in the South.*

The evidence is consistent with the hypothesis: The rules regulating city–suburban interaction differ decisively between the states of the Manufacturing Belt and those of the South. As Kotler observes, "The imperial growth of our cities has always required their political partnership with the state legislatures and the courts."[47] It appears that such a partnership was dissolved long ago in the industrial states. By the same token, the permissive annexation laws of the southern states (which share the common denominator of late industrialization) signal their continuing partnerships with city governments.

THE SOCIAL USES OF THE INDUSTRIAL CITIES

The legacy of the industrial metropolis is thus not only physical in character but political as well. Superimposed on the fine-grained

46. Allowing for ties in ranks, the Z-score equivalent for the rank-sum test is 6.0. The frequency distributions for the two regional classes are sufficiently skewed as to preclude the use of *t*-tests, which are valid only on the assumption of an underlying normal distribution. Hence the nonparametric test, which is described in Hubert M. Blalock, *Social Statistics,* second edition (New York: McGraw-Hill, 1972), pp. 255–260.

47. Milton Kotler, *Neighborhood Government* (Indianapolis: Bobbs-Merrill, 1969), p. 22.

TABLE 4-8
Annexation Laws in the Manufacturing Belt and the South (as of 1965)

Restrictiveness of annexation law, by Wheeler's rating		Southern states	Manufacturing Belt states
("Easy")	0	Arkansas, Kentucky, Mississippi, Oklahoma, Tennessee, Texas, Virginia	Indiana
	1	Louisiana	
	2	Arizona, New Mexico, North Carolina, West Virginia	Ohio
	3	Alabama, Florida, South Carolina	Illinois, Michigan, Pennsylvania, Wisconsin
	4		New Jersey
("Hard")	5	Georgia	Connecticut, Maryland, Massachusetts, New York, Rhode Island

ethnic differentiation of the turn-of-the-century city was a larger, market-generated polarization of core and periphery housing by income class. In the end, the decentralizing middle class succeeded in their quest for political autonomy from the regime of the industrial city. As a result, social and ethnic demarcations bred formal and permanently fixed local administrative lines.

It hardly needs saying that the old city's frozen borders continue to provide key regulatory services today. An unbroken chain links the polarized settlement patterns of the turn-of-the-century metropolis to the present. When the stream of low-wage foreign labor dried up, first with the disruptions of World War I, then in 1924 by law, the demand for cheap labor continued to outstrip the supply available in the industrial cities. With the mechanization of southern agriculture, uprooted blacks provided a major alternative source of unskilled labor for northern factories.

In other words, the end of the New Immigration triggered the first large-scale black migrations to northern cities. During World War I, through the boom of the 1920s, and again with the economy's recovery during World War II, the demand for low-wage industrial workers surged throughout the Manufacturing Belt. As an economist notes, the curtailment of the immigrant labor supply had domestic repercussions. . . . With the foreign labor supply largely cut off, periods of high labor demand in the North began increasingly to generate large movements of blacks out of the South. . . . With this shifting in the sources of labor supply, *the problem of assimilating immigrants was transformed into that of integrating blacks.*[48]

The burden of that problem, of course, would fall to the industrial cities. But the terms of the problem's "solution" had already been established, with the sealing of the industrial city's borders.

TERRITORIAL LEGACIES AND CITY ECONOMIC POSITIONS

State governments have been instrumental in the freezing of the borders of the industrial cities. The result today is that young cities include consistently larger shares of their urban-area populations than old ones. Such contrasts in territorial coverage merit further attention, because they highlight a key point for the assessment of economic redevelopment proposals.

As Table 4-1 illustrated, the average industrial city contained a mere 40% of its urbanized-area population in 1970, and only a single old city (Baltimore) could claim a clear majority of the larger population. On the other hand, the average young city included nearly three-quarters of its area's population. Although there was much variation from area to area, fully 8 of the 12 young cities covered more than two-thirds of the larger population.

To a surprising degree, a number of young cities thus resemble outright metropolitan, or areawide, governments. In it pure form, "metro" government has probably never been achieved in any twentieth-century American metropolis. But the fact that several of the young cities cover such large majorities of their urbanized-area populations makes them functional approximations of the ideal type. As a result of their far-flung territorial range, these central-city governments have extended *uniform tax rates* across much of their urban areas.

The other side of the coin is that the hemmed-in industrial cities have been left supremely vulnerable to suburban tax competition. In

48. Davis *et al., American Economic Growth,* p. 137. (Emphasis added.)

every older metropolis, central-city households and businesses can reduce their tax bills and maintain (or improve) their service levels just by leaving the city for its suburbs. This relationship lays the central city open to a continuing cycle of (a) flight of the tax base to low-tax suburbs, (b) a resulting upward pressure on city tax rates, and (c) continued erosion of the city base. The greater a city's annexation power, the greater its protection from this cycle. Just as the old city's frozen borders aggravate its already weak competitive position, so, too, does the young city's annexation power help it to preempt the organization of tax enclaves beyond its borders.

Annexation's influence on city growth is thus multifaceted. We saw in Chapter 3 the direct link: the generation of nominal growth in city population, that is, growth resulting from the redefinition of a city's territorial coverage. But city–suburban tax competition illustrates a second, and perhaps more important aspect of the relationship. Insofar as long-frozen borders give rise to sharp city–suburban tax differentials, annexation contrasts also shape *real* growth, meaning growth within any given territorial domain.

This issue is central to the next chapter's findings on city economic realignments. For jobs as for population, suburbanization has hit the tightly bounded industrial cities much harder than the territorially inclusive young cities. Part of this differential impact unquestionably reflects the young city's comparative protection from suburban tax competition. To that extent, the young city's advantages within the economic system are bolstered by its favorable institutional endowment. To that extent also, proposals for the old city's economic redevelopment should take account of the obstacles posed by local fiscal institutions—institutions around which the entire social system of the industrial metropolis is organized, and which will not soon change.

5

CITIES WITHIN THE INDUSTRIAL
SYSTEM

A rejuvenation, or jobs-to-people, approach to the urban problem
would attempt to arrest the secular erosion of the old city's employment base. As Table 5-1 shows, between 1948 and 1972 the old cities
all lost jobs in four key categories the Commerce Department periodi-
cally enumerates.[1] By contrast, all 12 young cities registered sizable
gains in these categories.

The feasibility of rejuvenation depends, of course, on the causes of
the industrial city's long-term job losses. Accordingly, this chapter
explores the reasons for the old city's economic decline during the key
transition period, the quarter-century leading up to 1972. The use of
1972 as an endpoint means that employment changes are being measured for roughly comparable phases of the business cycle, so that
they are truly secular in character. It also means, of course, that whatever manufacturing job losses occurred preceded the rise in energy
costs triggered by the 1973 oil embargo.

Our inquiry will suggest that city job losses can be traced to
realignments within the U.S. industrial system since 1945. During the

1. Manufacturing, wholesale trade, retail trade, and selected services employment,
each of which is counted every 5 years.

95

TABLE 5-1
Percentage Changes in Central-City Employment in Trade, Services, and Manufacturing:
1948–1972

Age class	City, by 1910 metropolitan size	Total[a]	Manufacturing	Selected services	Population: 1950–1970
Industrial	New York	− 11	− 19	+ 58	0
	Chicago	− 24	− 36	+ 48	− 7
	Philadelphia	− 27	− 38	+ 62	− 6
	Boston	− 23	− 42	+102	− 20
	Pittsburgh	− 27	− 23	+ 40	− 23
	St. Louis	− 38	− 44	+ 34	− 27
	San Francisco	− 8	− 29	+110	− 8
	Baltimore	− 15	− 25	+ 67	− 5
	Cleveland	− 31	− 38	+ 48	− 18
	Buffalo	− 30	− 39	+ 39	− 20
	Detroit	− 40	− 47	+ 13	− 18
	Cincinnati	− 17	− 29	+ 44	− 10
Anomalous	Los Angeles	+ 66	+ 68	+218	+ 43
	Washington	+ 3	+ 9	+ 94	− 6
	Milwaukee	− 12	− 21	+ 89	+ 12
	Kansas City	+ 11	+ 22	+ 91	+ 11
	New Orleans	+ 9	− 19	+140	+ 4
	Seattle	+ 24	+ 9	+126	+ 14
Young	Indianapolis	+ 33	+ 17	+ 95	+ 74
	Atlanta	+ 68	+ 40	+256	+ 50
	Denver	+ 52	+ 34	+204	+ 24
	Columbus	+ 59	+ 50	+161	+ 44
	Memphis	+ 69	+ 59	+136	+ 58
	Nashville	+125	+ 116	+167	+157
	Dallas	+148	+ 214	+262	+ 94
	San Antonio	+ 97	+ 96	+168	+ 60
	Houston	+178	+ 161	+396	+107
	Jacksonville	+119	+ 98	+202	+159
	San Diego	+160	+ 141	+363	+108
	Phoenix	+553	+1538	+785	+444
Means and significance of mean differences					
Industrial cities		− 24	− 34	55	− 14
Young cities		138	214	263	115
Difference		163	248	209	128
Significance		$p < .01$	$p = .07$	$p < .01$	$p < .001$

Source: U.S. Bureau of the Census, *Census of Manufactures: 1947 (Area Statistics); Census of Manufactures: 1972 (Area Statistics); Census of Business: 1948,* area statistics for retail trade, wholesale trade, and selected services; *Census of Business: 1972,* area statistics for retail trade, wholesale trade, and selected services.

[a] Includes wholesale and retail trade, selected services, and manufacturing.

booming war economy of the late 1960s, observers like Wilbur Thompson believed that the industrial cities could successfully convert from declining trade and manufacturing sectors to a growing services base, including, in particular, office employment. But the economic cross-currents of the 1970s have created serious doubts about a city's ability to rely on the services sector as its economic wellspring.

Illustrative of such doubts are Thompson's second thoughts, as voiced in 1975:

> Whatever [sic] happened to the post-industrial age that was supposed to strengthen our central cities? Ten years ago, we all talked optimistically about the new age of services. "Post-industrial" does not, of course, tell one what the new age is, but only what it isn't. What happened to this new force that was supposed to come in and rebuild the cores of our aging metropolises?[2]

One answer is that "post industrialism" is something that happens by default, merely an intersectoral employment shift reflecting productivity lags in services relative to manufacturing.[3] If so, then post-industrialism's fruits may prove sour, and a local (or national) economy's competitive position will continue to ride on its prowess in manufacturing. This chapter builds an empirical case to that effect, one ranging from cities to regions.

THE DETERMINANTS OF CENTRAL-CITY JOB CHANGES: 1948 – 1972

With few exceptions, studies of central-city economic changes have focused mainly on suburbanization.[4] If suburbanization were the last word, however, young cities could hardly have grown so rapidly since 1945. Nor, for that matter, could a city like New York have held

2. Wilbur Thompson, "Economic Processes and Employment Problems in Declining Metropolitan Areas," in *Post-Industrial America: Metropolitan Decline & Inter-Regional Job Shifts,* eds. George Sternlieb and James W. Hughes (New Brunswick, New Jersey: Center for Urban Policy Research, 1975), p. 191.

3. In oversimplified form, this is the message of Victor Fuchs' definitive study, *The Service Economy* (New York: National Bureau of Economic Research, 1968).

4. For a review of the literature, see Bennett Harrison, *Urban Economic Development* (Washington, D.C.: The Urban Institute, 1974), chapter 2.

its own, in employment terms, during the 1960s. Evidently other forces are at work, forces that can somehow moderate the impact of suburbanization.

What are these moderating influences, and why have they aided young cities more than old ones? By one account, that of Wilfred Lewis, Jr., the primary influences on specific cities have been the business cycle and the city's regional setting:

> Of the various major factors, it is by all odds the national growth rate that explains most of the difference between higher and lower employment growth in a given central city at different times. . . . Comparing different cities at the same time, it is the regional growth factor— i.e., whether the city is located in a fast-growing or slow-growing [SMSA]—that primarily accounts for whether employment growth . . . is high or low.[5]

Assessing city job performance over the 15 years before 1963, John F. Kain offered a complementary interpretation:

> Large increases in employment took place in most of the spacious, low-density central cities of rapidly growing Southern, Western, and Southwestern metropolitan areas. The explanation for these increases in central-city employment is, of course, the favorable confluence of high metropolitan growth rates and large tracts of unencumbered vacant land within city boundaries. Similarly, the older dense manufacturing cities of the East and Midwest experienced especially large declines.[6]

SUBURBANIZATION AND ITS OFFSETS

The implication is that a number of major determinants interact to shape city job changes. Suburbanization's toll on a central-city economy appears to vary (a) with the metropolitan growth rate, as well as (b) over the course of the national business cycle. Furthermore, as Kain's reference to city borders points up, this *political* variable determines the extent to which decentralization as an economic process translates into the more specific institutional outcome, suburbanization. In other words, both (c) initial boundary placement and (d) subsequent annexation activity can prevent the outward sweep of people and jobs from becoming a shift from a city to its suburbs.

5. Quoted in Harrison, *Urban Economic Development,* p. 32.
6. John F. Kain, "Postwar Changes in Land Use in the American City," in *Toward a National Urban Policy,* ed. Daniel P. Moynihan (New York: Basic Books, 1970), p. 75.

Abstracting from the temporary role of the business cycle and the transitory effects of initial boundary placement, we thus find two apparent long-term offsets to suburbanization. One is annexation, the expansion of municipal borders so as to keep rapidly growing peripheral territory within the central city's political dominion. The other is the metropolitan growth rate—which may vary in turn by region.

Table 5-2 gives an overview of the actual association between these two suggested determinants and city job changes. In view of the results of Chapter 3, the pattern of association should come as no surprise: By inspection, both annexation and areawide growth appear to favor young cities and penalize old ones. To put it another way, large increases in land area have occurred only in rapidly growing, younger metropolitan areas. Conversely, the industrial cities have been hampered both by frozen borders and by sluggish metropolitan growth. So either or both of the two suggested determinants could seemingly account for the life-cycle alignment of the city job changes.

THE PRIMACY OF THE METROPOLITAN GROWTH RATE

For a more specific reading, we might formally test the relationship between long-term city job changes, on the one hand, and changes in the values of the two determinants, on the other. Toward that end, define the 1948–1972 percentage changes in city jobs as J; the corresponding SMSA percentage change as M; and the 1950–1970 percentage changes in city land area as L.

Then the two determining variables explain over 90% of the variance in city job changes:

$$J = -46.6 + 1.0M + 0.03L, \tag{1}$$
$$ (6.0) \quad (15.8) \quad (3.2)$$
$$N = 30, \qquad SE = 31.7, \qquad R^2 = .93.$$

On average, a rise of one percentage point in SMSA job growth boosts a city's "predicted" job growth by the same amount. Surprisingly, for each 1-point rise in a city's 1950 land area, the predicted city growth rate rises by a minute .03 percentage points. Small as this latter estimate seems, the t-ratios listed beneath the coefficients indicate that the estimates are statistically reliable.

For our purposes, the equation's real interest resides in the signs—positive and negative—of the coefficient estimates. Just as for the

TABLE 5-2
Correlates of Employment Growth in the 30 Largest Cities: 1948–1972 (Percentage Changes)

Age class	City, by 1910 metropolitan size	Four categories of city employment, 1948-1972	Four categories of SMSA employment, 1948-1972	City territory, 1950-1970
Industrial	New York	− 11	3	0
	Chicago	− 24	21	7
	Philadelphia	− 27	15	0
	Boston	− 23	18	0
	Pittsburgh	− 27	−9	2
	St. Louis	− 38	18	0
	San Francisco	− 8	45	0
	Baltimore	− 15	30	0
	Cleveland	− 31	14	1
	Buffalo	− 30	3	5
	Detroit	− 40	15	0
	Cincinnati	− 17	27	4
Anomalous	Los Angeles	+ 66	119	3
	Washington	+ 3	149	0
	Milwaukee	− 12	21	90
	Kansas City	+ 11	49	292
	New Orleans	+ 9	55	0
	Seattle	+ 24	81	18
Young	Indianapolis	+ 33	37	587
	Atlanta	+ 68	146	256
	Denver	+ 52	155	42
	Columbus	+ 59	82	242
	Memphis	+ 69	81	108
	Nashville	+125	109	2208
	Dallas	+148	165	137
	San Antonio	+ 97	105	165
	Houston	+178	174	171
	Jacksonville	+119	108	2436
	San Diego	+160	235	219
	Phoenix	+553	503	1350
Means and significance of mean differences				
Industrial cities		− 24	17	2
Young cities		138	160	676
Difference		163	143	674
Significance		$p < .01$	$p < .01$	$p < .01$

Source: Columns 1 and 2: same as for Table 5-1. Column 3: same as for Table 3-2, Columns 2 and 3.

demographic equations tested in Chapter 3, the constant's negative sign means that it can be regarded as an index of suburbanization. Conversely, the positive coefficients signal offsets to suburbanization.

By way of illustration, Figure 5-1 portrays the neutralizing effects of a sufficiently rapid SMSA growth rate. The figure renders a "partial" regression line like the one developed in the last chapter to depict population changes. This line relates city to SMSA job growth on the assumption that city territory remains unchanged. In other words, municipal land area is treated as a fixed parameter.

The graph's y-intercept of -46.6% is, of course, the predicted job loss when SMSA job growth is statistically equated to zero. As the SMSA growth rate increases, the line of average relationship rises with a slope of 1.0—the size of the second coefficient estimate in the equation. Each 1% rise in the areawide growth rate thus increases the predicted value of the central city's job change by exactly one percentage point.

The graph describes how predicted city job losses are first damped down and then canceled out altogether at an SMSA growth rate of

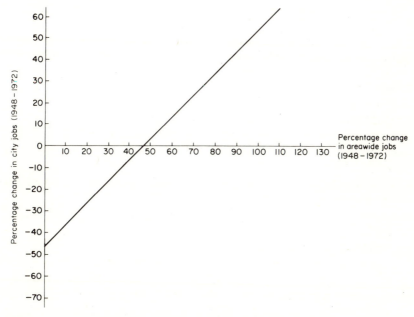

Figure 5-1. Rapid SMSA job growth as an offset to city job losses. [Based on Eq. (1).]

46.6%. At that value, the partial regression line crosses the x-axis—meaning that a city neither gains nor loses jobs over the course of the period. Above that point, the prediction is that the city actually gains new jobs, at a rate that rises steadily with the areawide growth rate.

How much does this partial view tell us about the actual distribution of city job gains and losses? For the industrial cities—the cities whose borders have not in fact changed for many decades—the diagram discloses a seemingly comprehensive explanation for their massive job losses. On one level, at least, the explanation is brutally simple. That is that the slow growth of the industrial metropolis as a whole has subjected the old central city to the full and devastating impact of job decentralization.

The other side of the coin is that even without annexation, many young cities would have gained jobs. After all, the median rate of job growth for the younger metropolis reached 127%. That is far more than twice the threshold rate of 47%, the rate above which a central city's predicted job change turns positive.

The Secondary Role of Annexation

Of course, every young city also enjoyed the advantages of annexation, typically on a scale large enough to double or triple its initial land area. This brings us to the next question. After allowing for the areawide growth rate, what role have such large-scale annexations had in the young city's vigorous job growth?

The answer turns on the size of the coefficient estimate for L, the annexation variable. In the first place, the estimate, .03, means that doubling a city's land area between 1950 and 1970 raises the city's predicted job growth by a scant 3 percentage points. The apparent explanation for this slight impact is that most large annexations have added relatively undeveloped territory to the young city's geographical domain. To that extent, annexation's stimulus to city job counts may not become manifest for several decades—or over an even longer period than the one measured here.

One should not overlook annexation's indirect benefits, as outlined in the last chapter. By extending a city's territorial domain, annexation can preempt the establishment of suburban tax enclaves. Insofar as annexation power dampens city–suburban tax competition in this way, a central city can attract or hold families and businesses. Here again, of course, the benefits of annexation may not accrue for some time after new territory is acquired.

In any case, the predicted "fits" for individual cities indicate that, in practice, the SMSA growth rate played the more powerful role. Table 5-3 lists the predicted rates of job growth for the 30 cities. For any given city, the predicted figure reflects the interplay of the constant (−46.6), on the one hand, and the computed offsets from annexation and SMSA growth, on the other. It may be seen by inspection that in most young cities, SMSA growth provided a considerably larger spur to city job gains than did annexation.

The upshot is that a central city's economic fate can be viewed as linked to that of its larger metropolitan area. Between 1948 and 1972, when the older metropolis generated relatively slow job growth, the old city lost jobs in the categories we have surveyed. During the 1970s, the older area stopped growing altogether, and its central city's economic prospects deteriorated further. The next section suggests that the reasons for this sequence lie in the older SMSA's loss of industrial competitiveness.

MANUFACTURING AND METROPOLITAN
JOB GROWTH

In the late 1960s Thompson suggested a strong positive link between metropolitan size and metropolitan growth, a link that has come to be described as "the ratchet effect":

> Growth creates size and size reacts to restructure the local economy so as virtually to ensure further growth at a near average rate—reacts, that is, to produce growth stability. . . . We would not expect to find the large diversified export sector generating unusually rapid growth or very slow growth. . . . A good case can be made that *each of the two dozen or so urban areas with a million to five million population will net out to about an average growth over the next fifty years, and more than double in size.*[7]

The prediction is notable both for its specificity and for its timing. It appeared just as a number of those two dozen areas were about to be hit by absolute declines in population and employment. Perceptions

7. Wilbur Thompson, "Internal and External Factors in the Development of Urban Economies," in *Issues in Urban Economics,* eds. Harvey S. Perloff and Lowdon Wingo, Jr. (Baltimore: Johns Hopkins Press, 1968), p. 52, p. 62. (Emphasis added.)

TABLE 5-3

Annexation and SMSA Job Growth as Offsets to Job Dispersion (Percentages)[a]

Age class	City, by 1910 metropolitan size	Residual	Predicted city job growth	Offset effects	
				SMSA job growth	Annexation
Industrial	New York	+ 33	− 44	3	0
	Chicago	+ 1	− 25	21	0
	Philadelphia	+ 5	− 32	15	0
	Boston	+ 6	− 29	18	0
	Pittsburgh	+ 29	− 56	−9	0
	St. Louis	− 9	− 29	18	0
	San Francisco	− 7	− 1	45	0
	Baltimore	+ 2	− 17	30	0
	Cleveland	+ 2	− 33	14	0
	Buffalo	+ 13	− 43	3	0
	Detroit	− 8	− 32	15	0
	Cincinnati	+ 2	− 19	27	0
Anomalous	Los Angeles	− 7	+ 73	119	0
	Washington	−100	+103	149	0
	Milwaukee	+ 10	− 22	21	3
	Kansas City	− 1	+ 12	49	10
	New Orleans	0	+ 9	55	0
	Seattle	− 11	+ 35	81	1
Young	Indianapolis	+ 23	+ 10	37	20
	Atlanta	− 40	+108	146	9
	Denver	− 58	+110	155	1
	Columbus	+ 15	+ 44	82	8
	Memphis	+ 24	+ 45	81	10
	Nashville	− 12	+137	109	74
	Dallas	+ 25	+123	165	5
	San Antonio	+ 33	+ 64	105	6
	Houston	+ 44	+134	174	6
	Jacksonville	− 25	+144	108	82
	San Diego	− 36	+196	235	7
	Phoenix	+ 50	+503	503	45

[a] Based on Eq. (1).

have changed accordingly, such that by 1976 the head of an Ohio-based research organization would say,

> It's been fashionable to talk about central cities as the hole in the metropolitan doughnut. . . . Now what you have is metropolitan populations themselves declining—in Akron or Cleveland—or barely holding their own, as in Detroit. You have to worry that the whole doughnut may be rotting.[8]

In retrospect, at least, the record of metropolitan employment growth prior to the 1970s discloses clear signs of the older area's impending economic stagnation. To be more precise, the record suggests that an underlying mechanism has generated contrasts in SMSA job growth, contrasts which, during the 1970s, have only assumed a more dramatic form.

Suppose, in the first place, that an area's total employment growth pivots specifically on the competitiveness of its manufacturing sector within the national and world economies. Suppose also that this competitive position varies with the timing of the area's formative economic development. Then we would expect to find:

1. A life-cycle pattern governing metropolitan job growth in manufacturing.
2. SMSA private-sector job growth varying accordingly.
3. In view of the regional structure of SMSA age contrasts, regional growth rates varying with the age of the region's principal metropolitan areas.

As the next few pages will show, the facts are consistent with just such a scenario.

THE STAGNATION OF THE OLDER SMSA's INDUSTRIAL BASE

Between 1947 and 1972, the industrial SMSAs failed to gain new manufacturing employment.[9] By one indicator, these areas had

8. Ralph Widner, quoted in Mark R. Arnold, "Ahead: A New 'War between the States,'" *The National Observer*, 2 October 1976.

9. All SMSA comparisons in the chapter refer to the territorial definitions given in the 1972 *Census of Business* and *Census of Manufactures*. Since most SMSAs included several more counties in 1972 than in the original 1950 definitions, job counts for the base years (1947 for manufacturing and 1948 for trade and services) had to be reconstructed. In some cases base-year data for counties not included in the initial SMSA

emerged from World War II as the most specialized and highly developed manufacturing centers within the economy. As noted in Chapter 2, in 1950, the dozen older SMSAs had distinctively high proportions—on average, 35%—of the urban work force in manufacturing jobs. (As Table 5-4 shows, the only notable exception to this heavy reliance on industrial production was San Francisco, the one older area lying outside the Manufacturing Belt.) By contrast, for younger urban areas, the average figure remained below 20%.

In these terms, the intervening years have witnessed an inverse relationship between a metropolitan area's industrial maturity and its industrial growth. Nationwide, the number of wage and salary workers in manufacturing grew by about one-third between 1947 and 1972.[10] But the median older SMSA actually lost manufacturing employment over the period. Together, the dozen older SMSAs suffered a net loss of 184,000 such jobs.

Meantime, the median younger SMSA more than doubled its initial job count in manufacturing. Thus, the initially less industrialized area has typically added manufacturing jobs at more than four times the rate of the economy as a whole. In the aggregate, the younger areas' gain of 640,000 new industrial jobs accounted for about one-seventh of the total U.S. increase.

In itself, of course, the failure of the mature industrial SMSAs to generate new manufacturing jobs does not mean that they stopped developing after World War II. During the past three decades, the job structure of the economy has been reshaped by the emergence of what Fuchs has termed the "first service economy," the hallmark of which has been a much faster expansion of tertiary than of secondary employment.[11] Perhaps the older areas have served as the focal centers of the postindustrial phase in the economy's evolution—just as they spearheaded the nation's industrial transformation after the Civil War.

---

units had been withheld to avoid disclosure of information for individual firms. Almost invariably the deleted job counts appear to have been too small to affect base-year figures, as rounded to one decimal point. If there is any remaining bias, it has led to slight undercounts in initial SMSA employment and thus to overestimates of percentage gains.

10. The increase in U.S. manufacturing employment between 1947 and 1972 was 33.1%.

11. *The Public Interest*, 2 (Winter 1966), pp. 7–17. See also his book, cited in Note 3 above.

TABLE 5-4
1950 Industrial Structure and Post-1950 Growth in 30 Large SMSAs

Age class	SMSA, by 1910 metropolitan size	Percentage of urbanized-area workforce in mfg., 1950	Percentage change in SMSA mfg. jobs, 1947–1972	Change in SMSA mfg. employment, 1947–1972 (thousands)
Industrial	New York	30.8	− 8.6	− 89
	Chicago	37.7	+ 6.0	+ 52
	Philadelphia	35.6	− 6.3	− 34
	Boston	28.7	− 5.1	− 19
	Pittsburgh	38.0	− 22.5	− 76
	St. Louis	33.8	+ 0.8	+ 2
	San Francisco	19.4	+ 11.7	+ 19
	Baltimore	30.9	+ 1.8	+ 3
	Cleveland	40.5	− 2.0	− 6
	Buffalo	39.7	− 17.5	− 32
	Detroit	46.9	− 2.6	− 15
	Cincinnati	33.4	+ 9.2	+ 13
Anomalous	Los Angeles	25.6	+121.2	+427
	Washington	7.4	+140.8	+ 32
	Milwaukee	42.9	+ 3.4	+ 7
	Kansas City	24.5	+ 50.6	+ 40
	New Orleans	15.6	+ 16.9	+ 8
	Seattle	19.8	+ 70.9	+ 45
Young	Indianapolis	33.1	+ 20.3	+ 21
	Atlanta	18.3	+113.1	+ 70
	Denver	16.8	+169.5	+ 60
	Columbus	25.0	+ 60.6	+ 38
	Memphis	20.5	+ 73.2	+ 27
	Nashville	22.9	+102.2	+ 36
	Dallas	18.4	+204.5	+155
	San Antonio	11.6	+ 91.4	+ 16
	Houston	21.4	+142.0	+ 94
	Jacksonville	13.1	+ 95.9	+ 14
	San Diego	15.7	+211.1	+ 44
	Phoenix	10.4	+871.6	+ 64
Means and significance of mean differences				
Industrial cities		34.6	− 2.9	
Young cities		18.9	179.6	(Not
Difference		15.7	182.5	computed)
Significance		$p<.001$	$p<.001$	

Source: Column 1: same as Table 2-1, Column 1. Columns 2 and 3: same as for Table 5-1.

MANUFACTURING AS THE KEY SMSA EMPLOYMENT SECTOR

In other words, it is possible that the mature metropolitan area's comparative advantage has shifted from industrial production to services activities. A simple test of that possibility is to regress job growth in an SMSA's services sector on changes in its manufacturing employment. More specifically, we might hypothesize that the manufacturing variable has governed job growth in the other private-sector categories we have surveyed—wholesale trade, retail trade, and selected services. Such a test should help clarify the spatial implications of the emergence of the postindustrial economy. Put plainly, the issue is whether the services sector has cut loose from the manufacturing base. Or, alternatively, is there the sort of binding linkage between the two sectors that traditional developmental perspectives might suggest?

The dependent variable can be designated S, for "services," where S denotes the 1948–1972 percentage changes in SMSA trade and services jobs. The independent variable, the 1947–1972 percentage changes in SMSA manufacturing employment, can be labeled I, for "industrial." (The values the variables have taken in the 30 SMSAs are listed in Table 5-5.) By ordinary least squares,

$$S = 61.6 + 0.44I, \qquad (2)$$
$$(9.5)\,(12.4)$$
$$N = 30, \qquad SE = 31.5, \qquad R^2 = .85.$$

From such a simple specification, these are rather striking results. A remarkable 85% of the variation in the growth of trade and services employment is explained by the change in SMSA manufacturing employment. Moreover, the coefficient estimates carry high t-ratios '(parenthesized, as usual, beneath the estimates), suggesting that the relationship is fairly uniform from one SMSA to the next.

Nevertheless, a scatter diagram of the observations for the 30 SMSAs reveals a problem with the coefficient estimates. (See Figure 5-2.) It appears that a single observation, the one for the Phoenix SMSA, has exerted a disproportionate influence on the regression estimates. Phoenix represents an "outlier," in the sense that its manufacturing growth rate far outstripped that of any other metropolitan area. As result, the observation for Phoenix weighs especially heavily on the regression line, pivoting it away from the locus of observations for the remaining 29 areas.

TABLE 5-5

Percentage Changes in SMSA Employment in Manufacturing and in Trade and Services, 1947–1972

Age class	City, by 1910 metropolitan size	I: Manu- facturing, 1947–1972	S: Trade and services, 1948–1972	M: Four categories combined
Industrial	New York	− 9	13	3
	Chicago	+ 6	41	21
	Philadelphia	− 6	50	15
	Boston	− 5	47	18
	Pittsburgh	− 22	15	−9
	St. Louis	+ 1	42	18
	San Francisco	+ 12	70	45
	Baltimore	+ 2	67	30
	Cleveland	− 2	43	14
	Buffalo	− 18	42	3
	Detroit	− 3	50	15
	Cincinnati	+ 9	54	27
Anomalous	Los Angeles	+121	117	119
	Washington	+141	150	149
	Milwaukee	+ 3	55	21
	Kansas City	+ 51	47	49
	New Orleans	+ 17	67	55
	Seattle	+ 71	90	81
Young	Indianapolis	+ 20	58	37
	Atlanta	+113	168	146
	Denver	+170	148	155
	Columbus	+ 61	105	82
	Memphis	+ 73	86	81
	Nashville	+102	115	109
	Dallas	+204	142	165
	San Antonio	+ 91	111	105
	Houston	+142	197	174
	Jacksonville	+ 96	114	108
	San Diego	+211	248	235
	Phoenix	+872	399	503
Means and significance of mean differences				
Industrial cities		− 3	45	17
Young cities		180	158	160
Difference		182	113	143
Significance		$p = .02$	$p < .01$	$p < .01$

Source: Same as for Table 5-1.

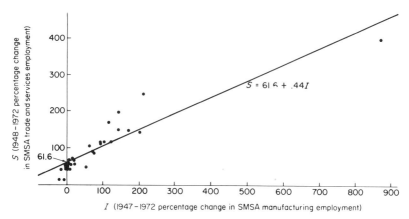

Figure 5-2. Scatter diagram: SMSA trade and services employment growth (%) as a function of SMSA percentage change in manufacturing employment.

To get a better measure of the structural relationship as it held for most SMSAs, the observation for Phoenix should be dropped, and the regression reestimated.[12] When this modification is made, the coefficient estimates change,

$$S = 46.6 + 0.73I, \tag{3}$$
$$(8.5)\,(11.9)$$
$$N = 29, \qquad SE = 22.6, \qquad R^2 = .84.$$

but the equation's explanatory power (as measured by the R^2) remains virtually the same.

National versus Local Influences on SMSA Services Growth

Judging by Eq. (3), growth rates for SMSA services employment have reflected both national and local influences. The fitted regression suggests that metropolitan areas have indeed shared in the post-industrial phase of the economy's development, but that the local manufacturing base remains the overriding determinant of an area's private-sector job growth.

By one reading of the equation. the postindustrial effect on SMSA services employment registers in the regression constant. Technically, the constant says that areas experiencing no change in manufacturing

---

12. A useful discussion of the theoretical and practical costs and benefits of dropping an outlier and reestimating a regression appears in G. S. Maddala, *Econometrics* (New York: McGraw-Hill, 1977), pp. 89–90.

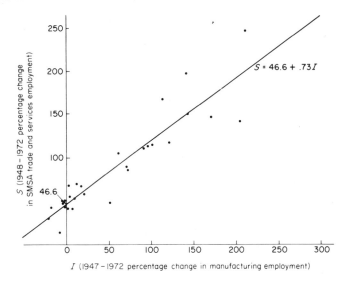

Figure 5-3. Scatter diagram for Eq. (3): Phoenix SMSA omitted.

employment should still have scored a 47% increase, on average, in trade and services employment. It is important to note that *the constant is independent of any specifically local factors*—whether manufacturing expansion or whatever. (Local influences other than the manufacturing variable all show up as "unexplained variation" in services growth rates.) Hence it can be read as a reflection of the rapid national expansion in tertiary employment, that is, of the postindustrial economy.

The empirical relevance of the old export-base view shows up in the coefficient for the manufacturing variable, and in the large R^2.[13] The coefficient estimate indicates that each 1-percentage-point rise in an SMSAs manufacturing employment was matched statistically by a rise of 0.73 percentage points in trade and services jobs. The R^2 of .84 measures the importance of the manufacturing variable as compared with any other *local* influences on services expansion. It says that all but about 16% of the variation in services growth can be attributed to variations in local industrial performance.

Which counted more, then, the "postindustrial" or the "industrial" component? To judge from the large constant, the rapid national expansion in services employment was by no means trivial as an influence on SMSA employment growth. Nevertheless, job growth in the

13. A review and critique of the export base literature appears in Werner Z. Hirsch, *Urban Economic Analysis* (New York: McGraw-Hill, 1973), pp. 186–194.

services sector did vary tremendously among the 30 SMSAs, ranging from a meager 13% for the New York SMSA to well over 200% in Jacksonville (and, of course, in Phoenix).

This pattern of differential employment growth in the services sector has been shaped for the most part by varying rates of job creation in the manufacturing sector. In particular, areas that failed to generate new manufacturing jobs also registered below-average gains in trade and services employment. In terms of the issue raised earlier, the industrially mature SMSAs have *not* benefited from a new comparative advantage in services activities.

THE FALL OF THE HEARTLAND

In sum, the old city's job losses have clear and specific sources. The key lies in the older SMSA's industrial malaise. Over the quarter-century after 1947, the giant older areas—the nation's traditional manufacturing centers—failed to generate new manufacturing jobs. As a result, their central cities experienced a massive suburbanization of manufacturing employment. Over the long haul, city job losses in trade and manufacturing were not fully compensated by gains in the services sector.

City, metropolis—and what of the region? The industrially stagnant SMSAs are, of course, clustered within the Manufacturing Belt, which ranges from Boston to Baltimore to St. Louis to Milwaukee. This concluding section assesses the damage the older area's industrial troubles have inflicted on the heartland region as a whole.

FROM RELATIVE TO ABSOLUTE DECLINE

From the dawn of American industrialization until after World War II, the Northeast and Upper Midwest enjoyed an unchallenged hegemony within the U.S. economy. But since the mid-1960s this core region has been hit by absolute losses in manufacturing employment—even as the rest of the nation has registered sizable gains. The timing and pace of this shift can be gleaned from a few basic indicators.

Relative Industrial Decline: Before 1970

The Manufacturing Belt had already lost its relative industrial preeminence by 1970. From 1909 until 1947, the belt's share of U.S.

manufacturing employment fell only slightly, from 73.0 to 68.2%.[14] But by 1969 (the peak historical year for the core's manufacturing employment), this share had fallen off sharply, to 56.3%. Although employment is only a partial indicator of regional positions, value-added data tell essentially the same story. In short, the core's relative decline awaited World War II, then occurred at a fairly rapid rate during the 1950s and 1960s.

Manufacturing Jobs Preceded Population

Under the traditional division of labor, the core region claimed nearly half again as much U.S. manufacturing employment as it had of the nation's population. Between 1947 and 1969, however, the belt's share of U.S. manufacturing employment declined much more rapidly than did its population share (which fell by only about 3 percentage points). Hence the *ratio* of the two shares fell from 1.46 in 1947 to 1.28 in 1969, a trend that has accelerated sharply during the 1970s.[15] The regional dispersion of manufacturing jobs has thus occurred at a much faster pace than the redistribution of population.

The Year 1966 as an Historical Divide

As Figure 5-4 discloses, the core region's relative decline gave way to absolute job losses in the manufacturing sector after 1969. But the figure also reveals an earlier and unambiguous tendency toward stagnation after 1966. In the midst of a superheating war economy that would generate roughly a million new manufacturing jobs between 1966 and 1969, the core region added a comparatively meager 150,000 jobs to its manufacturing payrolls. Then, between 1969 and 1977, the Manufacturing Belt lost over 1.3 million manufacturing jobs.[16] The heartland's relative decline in the manufacturing sector had turned to absolute decline, in a pattern the recovery of the late 1970s would not fully compensate.

14. See Robert Estall, *A Modern Geography of the United States* (Chicago: Quadrangle Books, 1972), p. 291. Data for more recent comparisons are from U.S. Bureau of Economic Analysis, *Long Term Economic Growth, 1860–1970* (Washington, D.C.: U.S. Government Printing Office, 1973); Bureau of Labor Statistics, *Employment and Earnings*, various issues; and Bureau of the Census, *Current Population Reports*, Series P-25.

15. See the sources cited in Note 14.

16. U.S. Bureau of Labor Statistics, *Employment and Earnings*, various issues.

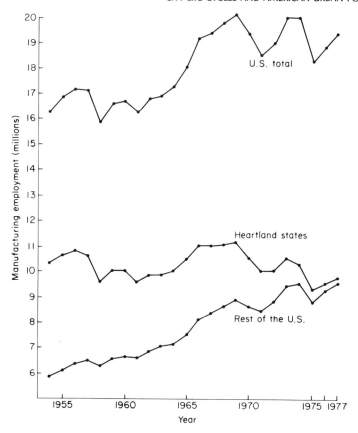

Figure 5-4. Manufacturing employment growth in the heartland and periphery: 1954 – 1977.

POSTINDUSTRIALISM'S SHORTCOMINGS

What the heartland lost, the rest of the nation gained: some 1.5 million manufacturing jobs in the period 1966–1977. And "the rest of the nation" means just that: not only the Southern Rim, but also the states of the Mountains, Plains, and Far West. It means, in other words, the economy's traditional periphery, or hinterland.

Table 5-6 provides a more fine-grained picture of the core–periphery shift since 1966.[17] Not coincidentally, California plays a

17. See "A New Layer of Structural Unemployment," *Business Week*, 14 November 1977, for a map of manufacturing employment changes aggregated by region for the period 1966–1977.

TABLE 5-6
Percentage Changes In State Tertiary Job Growth and State Manufacturing Job Growth, 1966–1977

State	Manufacturing employment	Services employment	State	Manufacturing employment	Services employment
1. New York	−24.0	9.5	25. S. Carolina	16.9	74.3
2. Maryland	−17.0	45.0	26. Minnesota	16.9	51.0
3. Connecticut	−15.6	42.7	27. Virginia	17.2	58.7
4. Pennsylvania	−14.6	26.8	28. Tennessee	17.3	51.7
5. New Jersey	−13.7	39.1	29. Nebraska	17.5	42.0
6. Massachusetts	−13.7	26.2	30. Oregon	17.9	54.2
7. Illinois	−12.9	24.6	31. Alabama	18.5	44.5
8. Maine	−12.5	53.4	32. Kansas	20.0	47.0
9. Rhode Island	−6.7	27.1	33. N. Carolina	25.4	56.8
10. Washington	−6.2	55.3	34. Kentucky	25.8	48.9
11. W. Virginia	−5.3	32.5	35. Wyoming	27.9	60.3
12. Ohio	−3.8	40.1	36. Florida	30.2	85.1
13. Missouri	−3.7	23.5	37. Mississippi	35.3	58.7
14. Vermont	−3.0	49.5	38. Arkansas	39.7	50.5
15. Montana	−2.0	53.8	39. Texas	40.5	62.1
16. Indiana	−1.9	39.2	40. Arizona	42.7	97.2
17. Michigan	−0.6	39.1	41. Colorado	43.0	70.4
18. Delaware	1.1	37.2	42. Oklahoma	42.5	54.7
19. New Hampshire	2.3	59.2	43. Utah	43.2	65.9
20. Wisconsin	3.4	59.2	44. N. Dakota	52.1	51.7
21. California	10.1	52.0	45. S. Dakota	57.2	54.7
22. Iowa	10.7	36.0	46. Idaho	61.0	71.8
23. Georgia	13.7	66.2	47. N. Mexico	66.3	55.8
24. Louisiana	16.6	41.3	48. Nevada	87.7	94.6

Source: U.S. Bureau of Labor Statistics, *Employment and Earnings*, various issues.

pivotal role in this broad regional realignment. All the 29 (contiguous) states adding manufacturing jobs at a rate above California's 10% gain lay outside the heartland. Every state in the core fell below this rate— and an imposing majority sustained actual losses, ranging to New York state's precipitous 24% decline. So even allowing for the gaining states' small initial bases (and thus for the ambiguity of their large percentage increases), the dichotomy is almost as sharply drawn in terms of signs, that is, gainers and losers.

The Link between Service and Manufacturing Jobs, by State

Just as at the metropolitan scale, one might ask whether the core states' job losses in manufacturing have been offset or amplified by tendencies in the services sector. On this question, Figure 5-5 is instructive. The figure reveals a tendency for states losing manufacturing jobs to have below-average growth in services employment.

The figure is based on a regression attributing half the recent variation in services job growth to the manufacturing variable:

$$S = 42.9 + 0.5M, \qquad\qquad (4)$$
$$(20.3)\ \ (6.8)$$
$$N = 48, \qquad SE = 12.4, \qquad R^2 = .50,$$

where S represents 1966–1977 percentage changes in tertiary sector employment, and M the corresponding state manufacturing change. (Values for both variables appear in Table 5-6.)

Relative to the SMSA equations fitted earlier, manufacturing's influence on services job growth is less decisive. In other words, at least one important explanatory variable has been omitted from Eq. (4). Still, the t-ratio for the manufacturing variable testifies to a statistically stable relationship between the industrial and service sectors.

Together, the table and the scatter plot confirm this broad impression of a systematic correspondence. The only state in the quadrant from Massachusetts to Maryland to Missouri to Illinois gaining any manufacturing jobs was Delaware, with a 1% rise. In turn (and as can be verified from the table or the diagram), no state in the quadrant registered growth in services jobs apace with the unweighted 48-state average. Conclusion: Manufacturing job losses by the core states have not been compensated by rapid job growth in services.

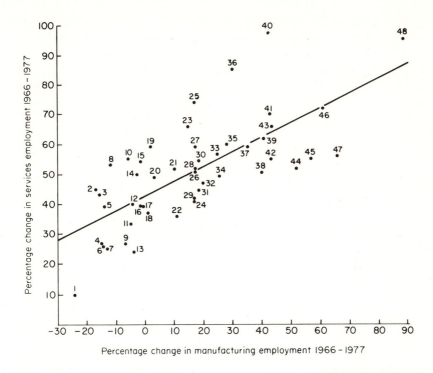

Figure 5-5. State tertiary job growth as a function of state manufacturing job growth: 1966 – 1977.

STATE CODES

1 – New York	13 – Missouri	25 – South Carolina	37 – Mississippi
2 – Maryland	14 – Vermont	26 – Minnesota	38 – Arkansas
3 – Connecticut	15 – Montana	27 – Virginia	39 – Texas
4 – Pennsylvania	16 – Indiana	28 – Tennessee	40 – Arizona
5 – New Jersey	17 – Michigan	29 – Nebraska	41 – Colorado
6 – Massachusetts	18 – Delaware	30 – Oregon	42 – Oklahoma
7 – Illinois	19 – New Hampshire	31 – Alabama	43 – Utah
8 – Maine	20 – Wisconsin	32 – Kansas	44 – North Dakota
9 – Rhode Island	21 – California	33 – North Carolina	45 – South Dakota
10 – Washington	22 – Iowa	34 – Kentucky	46 – Idaho
11 – West Virginia	23 – Georgia	35 – Wyoming	47 – New Mexico
12 – Ohio	24 – Louisiana	36 – Florida	48 – Nevada

In sum, for states and regions as for SMSAs, postindustrialism is no substitute for a competitive manufacturing sector. When the core's post-1945 relative industrial decline turned absolute after 1969, and its states lost manufacturing jobs in huge numbers, no unusual service-sector growth took up the slack. If anything, contrasts in state manufacturing growth gave rise to corresponding changes in the services sector.

What remains to be explained, of course, is the *reason* for the virtual industrial collapse of the older SMSAs—and with them the heartland—since the late 1960s.

6

THE PRODUCT CYCLE AND THE REJUVENATION QUESTION

We have yet to specify the causal mechanisms responsible for the job losses that have plagued the industrial cities since 1945. The last chapter provided the empirical groundwork for an appraisal of this issue. It disclosed that long-term city job losses can be traced to the industrial eclipse of the older metropolis. In turn, the older area's industrial collapse has shaken the entire heartland region, creating first relative and then (after 1969) absolute declines in the region's manufacturing employment. The forces shaping the old city's economic position thus extend to the regional scale, and perhaps beyond.

Whereas the technology of the industrial revolution encouraged the concentration of production in a core region, subsequent technologies have gradually cut all such centralizing ties. As a result, "Events once endemic to the metropolitan level, in particular employment decentralization, appear to have been attenuated to new spatial scales and are now working themeselves out over the entire geography of the country."[1] A new spatial regime is emerging, one dominated by a general decentralization of manufacturing.

1. George Sternlieb and James Hughes, "New Regional and Metropolitan Realities of America," *Journal of the American Institute of Planners*, 43:3 (July 1977), p. 231.

This new decentralized regime is the broad locational context within which a rejuvenation strategy would succeed or fail. Can concerted governmental action counter the dispersive trend and restore the older area's industrial position? The purpose of the chapter is to make use of a model explaining the dispersion of manufacturing so as to provide perspective on this question.

CORES, CYCLES, AND THE DECENTRALIZATION OF PRODUCTION

Numerous causes have been suggested for the regional economic shifts taking place within the U.S., causes ranging from oil, to sunshine, to business climates, to federal spending, to the emergence of a so-called information economy.[2] Withal, one might conclude that when it comes to the decentralization of production, whether domestic or worldwide, "Practice is ahead of theory and policy."[3]

The interpretation to be offered here emphasizes the technological dimension. But it also leaves room for other influences, both subjective (e.g., the business climate) and more traditional (e.g., labor costs).

The main idea, one introduced in Chapter 1, is that innovation provides a market-generated means of economic rejuvenation at a variety of spatial scales: urban, regional, and national. But when innovative capacity weakens, the centrifugal tendencies that are always present in interdependent economies become predominant.

This view is best known in regard to the world economy, which is also characterized by highly developed centers or cores, on the one hand, and peripheries, on the other. Viewing the deteriorating U.S. balance of trade after 1970 (but before OPEC), C. P. Kindleberger wrote of an economy-wide aging process,

> a slowing down of American economic vitality and elan—a climacteric in the life of the economy and perhaps society, such as Britain experienced in the last quarter of the nineteenth century when it was over-

2. See, for example, Kirkpatrick Sale, *Power Shift: The Rise of the Southern Rim and Its Challenge to the Eastern Establishment* (New York: Random House, 1975); *Business Week,* "The Second War Between the States," 17 May 1976, pp. 92–114; and Marc Porat, *The Information Economy.*

3. Steven Hymer, "The Multinational Corporation and the Law of Uneven Development," in *Economics and World Order: From the 1970's to the 1990's,* ed. Jagdish Bhagwati (New York: The Free Press, 1972), p. 115.

taken by Germany and the United States as we are now being overtaken by Japan.[4]

The key symptom of this climacteric is "The dynamic failure of the economy to produce *new exports to replace those now being eroded by the product cycle.*"[5] This perspective on the aging and renewal of economic systems provides the framework we need to sort out the rejuvenation issue.

We will find that a gradual dispersal of innovative capacity has weakened the capacity of the older metropolis to spawn new industries—in other words, to generate new product cycles. In consequence, both the older areas and the heartland as a whole have been rendered highly vulnerable to the loss of mature fabricating industries to the periphery and abroad.

From this standpoint, and considering the national and even global sources of the old city's job losses, a rejuvenation strategy would seem less realistic than one based on the dispersal of the minority poor away from the industrial cities.

THE CORE AND THE PERIPHERY IN RETROSPECT

By way of background, it will prove helpful to recall the traditional regional division of labor—the spatial system under which the Manufacturing Belt flourished for a century. Once the pillars of this traditional system have been isolated, the causes of more recent realignments can be easily discerned.

As noted in Chapter 1, the industrial revolution had a dramatic regional structure. Industrialization per se was concentrated within the Manufacturing Belt, which encompassed vital coal and iron deposits.[6] By contrast, the rest of the nation remained rural and resource-oriented. In 1890, barely 10% of the South's labor force held manufacturing jobs, as compared with more than a third in the Middle Atlantic region and nearly half in New England. Instead, both the

---

4. In a letter to the *New York Times,* 1 March 1973.

5. *Ibid.* (Emphasis added.)

6. A precise delineation of the Manufacturing Belt appears in David Ward, *Cities and Immigrants: A Geography of Change in Nineteenth-Century America* (New York: Oxford University Press, 1971), pp. 42–43.

defeated South and the remote West served as agricultural producers and raw-materials processors for the core's burgeoning markets.[7]

REGIONAL INDUSTRIAL ROLES, 1900–1950

During the first half of the twentieth century, the manufacturing that did develop in the periphery tended to be closely tied to specific resource endowments. In the meantime, the core performed most of the economy's fabricating activities, including the production of a broad spectrum of goods to be "exported" to the periphery.

Consider, in this regard, an historian's observations on the economy of a key periphery state:

> The economy of Texas... was and is colonial.... Texas began and remained a vast agrarian-mining complex, never developing a truly integrated economy.... Texans imported everything, whether Colt revolvers or Cadillacs, against the export of their raw, or slightly processed commodities. The so-called Texas industries... are really processing industries, whether baling cotton, packing beef, or cracking petroleum.[8]

Under the traditional division of labor, the diversified industrial core region enjoyed certain pronounced advantages. Most obvious perhaps was a generally higher standard of living—a reflection, in part, of the core's high productivity levels and correspondingly high wages. But the underlying advantage stemmed from the core's specialization in fabricating industries. Such fabricating industries as machinery and metals have grown much faster throughout this century than resource-processing industries like leather or tobacco products.

THE TENDENCY TOWARD REGIONAL DECENTRALIZATION

But despite its favorable industrial mix, the belt's hegemony was precarious. The core was always vulnerable to the flight of its labor-intensive (e.g., nondurables) manufacturing to the low-wage areas of

7. See Harvey Perloff and Lowdon Wingo, Jr., "Natural Resource Endowment and Regional Economic Growth," in *Regional Policy: Readings in Theory and Applications*, eds. John Friedmann and William Alonso (Cambridge: MIT Press, 1975), pp. 307–331.

8. T. R. Fehrenbach, "Seven Keys to Understanding Texas," *The Atlantic Monthly*, March 1975, p. 124.

the periphery. The historic drift of the shoe and textile industries away from New England, and of apparel manufacturing from New York to the Carolinas, are so familiar as to need no comment. But they illustrate an extraordinarily general issue. Once certain conditions crystallized in a fabricating industry within the core, *considerations of both cost and labor control encouraged the migration of the industry* to less developed (i.e., low-wage, nonunion) sites in the periphery.

The obvious question is how, in the face of such competition, the Manufacturing Belt could retain its industrial hegemony for so long. In retrospect, it is clear that a key factor sustaining its position (and differentiating it from the periphery) was the core region's capacity to adapt to changes in the economic environment.

In part, this capacity stemmed from the region's diversified industrial structure, so different from the narrow resource-related specializations characteristic of the periphery. But it also reflected the systematic practical knowledge—the technology—that was uniquely available to the Manufacturing Belt's firms, including individual entrepreneurs as well as corporate giants.

MACHINE TOOLS AND THE AMERICAN SYSTEM OF MANUFACTURES

Well into the twentieth century, in fact, the belt enjoyed a virtual monopoly on U.S. technological innovation. Nathan Rosenberg, in a definitive account of the nineteenth-century "American system of manufactures," has documented the extent of the regional concentration of technical know-how.[9] By way of background, and as he explained, a single industry served as the technological wellspring for the development of industry after industry, from firearms and sewing machines to bicycles and automobiles. This fundamental technological source was the machine-tools industry. In a time when technology had minimal links with the world of science, the machine-tools industry served as a repository of practical problem-solving lore. In other words, the industry's development was a prerequisite to the development of the American system—the system that began with the use of interchangeable parts for the production of rifles in the 1830s and led eventually to Ford's 1913 assembly line.

9. Nathan Rosenberg, *Technology and American Economic Growth* (New York: Harper & Row, 1972).

Spatially, the machine-tools industry was contained entirely within the Manufacturing Belt. Estimates published in 1914, for example, reported that one in five of the industry's 570 firms was located in Ohio, while all the rest could be found elsewhere in the belt.[10] As might be expected, this complete spatial correspondence derived from the fact that the industry's market, that is, producers of fabricated goods, was so heavily concentrated within the core region. The dramatic regional concentration of technical know-how helps explain how the belt retained its industrial hegemony for so long. *Innovative capacity as a source of industrial rejuvenation* was the key factor Perloff and Wingo ascribed to the core region, "the industrial seedbed of the economy. The newer products tend to be started here, nourished along, and as they find wide acceptance and volume grows, often the manufacturers find that they can supply the outlying markets more economically by producing on a decentralized basis."[11]

In short, and as the summary list in Table 6-1 suggests, the belt's traditional industrial hegemony reflected its ability to spawn new industries so as to offset the dispersion of its standardized fabricating operations to the periphery. By the same token, of course, the belt's more recent industrial malaise can be read as an indication that its innovative capacity has diminished to the point that the exodus of standardized operations has become the decisive factor.

To explore this possibility further, it will prove useful to recast the argument in somewhat more systematic terms, using the product-cycle model of industrial growth and decline.

THE PRODUCT CYCLE AND THE SEEDBED FUNCTION

In separate historical studies published in the 1930s, Simon Kuznets and Arthur Burns each concluded that individual industries tended to pass through a regular developmental cycle.[12] By the early 1940s, their findings had become codified as *the law of industrial growth*, a tendency (as one textbook put it) for industries to experience

10. *Ibid.*, p. 102.
11. Perloff and Wingo, "National Resource Endowment," p. 329.
12. Simon Kuznets, *Secular Movements in Production and Prices* (Boston: Houghton Mifflin, 1930); Arthur F. Burns, *Production Trends in the United States* (New York: National Bureau of Economic Research, 1934).

TABLE 6-1
Regional Industrial Roles: 1870–1950

Stylized characteristics	The Manufacturing Belt[a]	The periphery[b]
Nineteenth-century specialization:	Manufacturing	Agriculture and extraction
Timing of urbanization:	Pre-World War I	After World War I
Twentieth-century manufacturing:	Diversified mix of fabricating activities	Narrow specialization in resource-processing industries
Wage, income, and price levels:	High	Low
Technological position:	Seedbed for innovations (especially via machine-tools)	Recipient via diffusion
Basis of growth:	Specialization in new, rapidly growing industries	Competitive gains in standardized fabricating lines
Nature of vulnerability:	Dispersion of standardized operations to low-wage sites in the periphery	Initial specializations in stagnant, resource-oriented industries
Expected empirical (shift-share) correlates:	Positive mix, negative competitive effects	Negative mix, positive competitive effects

Source: Subjective classification, based on Perloff and Wingo, as cited in text.
[a] As approximated by the New England, Middle Atlantic, and East North-Central divisions.
[b] The rest of the continental economy, except for the "subnucleation" of California.

"a period of experimentation, a period of rapid growth, a period of diminished growth, and a period of stability or decline."[13]

This stylized product-cycle was said to reflect the interplay between the scale of output and the rate of technological progress within individual firms:

> As a result of the period of experimentation, both the product and the process have been materially improved as the industry enters its second phase of growth. The growth is further accelerated by reduction

13. E. B. Alderfer and H. E. Michl, *Economics of American Industry* (New York: McGraw-Hill, 1942), p. 14.

in the price of the product and by improvements in the marketing of it. One improvement leads to another, and the price is further reduced.... The industry passes next to the third stage, diminished growth. The rate of technical progress begins to slacken.... Usually only refinements of existing processes are effected.[14]

More recently, and as a first step in the virtual rediscovery of the model after years of neglect, Raymond Vernon emphasized the spatial aspects of any new industry's developmental cycle.[15] Although he related technological progress to scale, he also stressed the changing importance of "external economies," during the course of the product's standardization, a change that tended to render production footloose. Vernon's observations parallel those of Perloff and Wingo, and are very much to the point of the argument:

> As there arise new industries of the sort which require external economies in their early stages, the chances seem high that the [New York Metropolitan] Region will be a favored location at first; then as maturity sets in, these industries are likely to spread out to lower-cost locations. As new technologies develop which allow existing external-economy industries to "decompose" their processes and to transfer some of them to another area, they too will join in the outward move. But *one can only guess at the speed of these processes of birth and maturity and technological shifts.*[16]

During the 1960s, Vernon's students brought this perspective to bear on the question of international competitive positions and on the behavior of the multinational firm. In particular, Seev Hirsch, an Israeli planner, systematized the model's spatial implications. In a 1967 work, *The Location of Industry and International Competitiveness,* Hirsch suggested that mature industries in developed countries constituted fair game for less developed counties (LDCs).[17]

Hirsch reasoned that the third (mature) stage of the product cycle is characterized by stable technology, long production runs, and a reliance less on technical or managerial talent than on unskilled and semiskilled labor. By this reckoning LDCs could successfully compete

14. *Ibid.,* p. 15.

15. See Vernon, "International Investment and International Trade in the Product Cycle," *Quarterly Journal of Economics,* 1966, pp. 190–207.

16. Vernon, *Metropolis 1985* (Cambridge: Harvard University Press, 1960), p. 109. (Emphasis added.)

17. New York: Oxford University Press.

with the developed industrial nations as sites for mature fabricating industries. On the other hand, Hirsch saw the second (growth) phase as the natural specialization of a large developed economy like the U.S.

Since 1969, and especially during the severe recession of the mid-1970s, tendencies in the world economy seem to bear out Hirsch's argument. As Jan Tumlir and Richard Blackhurst, two economists with the General Agreement on Tariffs and Trade (GATT), have observed, manufacturing output failed to increase in the developed world between 1974 and 1976. Meantime industrial output in LDCs rose at average annual rate of fully 6%. Furthermore, even in the *prior* 4 years, 1969–1973, LDC manufacturing output grew nearly twice as fast as that of the developed world.[18]

What do such global realignments have to do with the regional issue? With the product cycle in mind, one could view LDCs as benefiting from a characteristic advantage in standardized manufacturing activities. Just as with the American periphery, the low labor costs and favorable "business climates" of such LDCs as South Korea and Taiwan attract the branch plants of multinational firms, whose hallmark is the capacity to shift production operations quickly.

By the same token, our depiction of the traditional regional relationship can now be restated in the parlance of the product cycle. That is, the weakness of the core region during its period of hegemony lay in its mature fabricating industries—industries that had reached the third stage of the product cycle and were therefore exportable. The Manufacturing Belt's ability to offset the dispersion of such industries depended on its capacity to generate new product cycles (new rounds of innovation and development) and to hold production through the growth phase.

THE DISPERSION OF THE SEEDBED FUNCTION

The product cycle thus suggests a general framework within which to interpret the decentralization of production at several spatial scales. At the regional scale, we have seen that the key lies in the balance between the core's seedbed function and the dispersion of stan-

18. "Why the Industrial Nations Aren't Growing," *Business Week,* 21 November 1977, pp. 138 *et seq.*

dardized (mature-industry) operations. Two empirical questions follow naturally from this observation:

1. Has innovative capacity spread throughout the spatial system, such that new, rapid-growth industries are no longer unique to the Manufacturing Belt?
2. Has the flight of standardized production from the core to the periphery accelerated?

EVIDENCE ON THE TRANSITION

In a paper exploring these questions, Rees and Norton found that both processes have been instrumental in the heartland's industrial decline.[19] As noted in the last chapter, the core region's relative decline accelerated during the 1960s and then turned absolute after 1969. By 1977, in fact, most heartland states had barely regained the levels of manufacturing employment of a decade before. Rees and Norton linked this decline to a sequence in which an accelerated loss of standardized operations was followed by a weakening of the core's ties to the economy's faster-growing industries.

While the heartland retained a favorable mix of new and expanding industries during the 1960s, the exodus of standardized operations swamped that advantage. (Here as throughout the chapter, incidentally, "exodus," "flight," and similar terms refer *not* to literal plant relocations, but only to sharply faster rates of industrial growth in decentralized locations.) Between 1963 and 1972, in fact, the core lagged behind the nation's rate of increase to the extent of fully a million manufacturing jobs. Then, during the 1970s, the link between the core and the seedbed function all but disappeared. For the years 1972–1976, the core's industrial specialties had slower rates of national growth than did manufacturing generally. To some extent, that probably reflected the 1975 recession's impact on the core's characteristic industries. But on balance, the evidence seems to suggest that the heartland was losing its traditional source of industrial rejuvenation—its ability to spawn and hold the economy's growth industries. As if to underscore this tendency, the periphery as a unit

19. R. D. Norton and John Rees, "The Product Cycle and the Spatial Decentralization of American Manufacturing," *Regional Studies*, forthcoming 1979. Parts of this chapter are drawn from the Norton and Rees article.

registered a positive net mix effect during the same period, signifying that its aggregated industrial mix was weighted toward the economy's faster-growing industries.

The upshot is that the natural dispersion of mature or standardized activities has accelerated—and is no longer being significantly offset by the spawning of new industries in the core. By the late 1970s, the economy's traditionally polarized industrial structure had given way to a virtually uniform distribution of manufacturing employment as between the core and periphery. Sufficient import-substitution had occurred in the periphery to strip the heartland of its specialized role, leaving only the Great Lakes area with anything like its prior position.

THE DECENTRALIZATION OF INNOVATIVE CAPACITY

One reason for this new regional relationship is the cumulative dispersion of innovative capacity. We have focused on the balance between innovation, a source of industrial rejuvenation, and product standardization, which permits the exporting of production from any specialized industrial core. As noted at the outset, a variety of influences have built up to alter that balance. But from the rejuvenation standpoint, the one that looms especially large is the rise of new industrial sources of innovation.

The key industrial sources of innovation now are the "science-based" industries, notably electronics and chemicals.[20] And in contrast to the machine-tools industry, these newer source industries tend to be widely dispersed throughout the economy, in accordance with regional resource endowments. A good illustration of the shift and of its importance is Texas, the nation's leading gainer in manufacturing employment in the decade after 1967. By virtue of its sunshine and oil—and the federal contracts, aerospace industry, and scientists they have helped attract since 1940—the state has come to specialize not only in petrochemicals but also in electronics. Following the precedent set by California, the first subnucleation, Texas has therefore become something of a seedbed in its own right. As such, it has spawned a

20. From a list of 277 major U.S. innovations between 1953 and 1973, the two-digit SIC industry group accounting for the largest number was SIC 36, electronics. Second was chemicals, SIC 28. Together, the two groups accounted for 98 innovations, or more than a third of the total. See National Science Board, *Science Indicators 1976* (Washington, U.S. Government Printing Office, 1977), p. 269.

series of innovations that have had an international impact during the 1970s.[21]

The rise of Texas as a global technological center symbolizes the new regional relationship. It also serves as a warning that the economy's geographical momentum runs counter to the logic of a rejuvenation strategy. Of course, some would argue that this "momentum" is largely the result of public policy—and hence that it could be redirected should the political will manifest itself. In response to this viewpoint, we might now take note of a systematic political barrier to the rejuvenation strategy.

21. As if to illustrate the resource connection, Texas Instruments (the source of a seemingly endless stream of innovations during the 1970s) can trace its origins to a group of Northeastern engineers who came to Texas to apply seismic-wave techniques to petroleum exploration. For an account of the company's success in generating innovations, see "Texas Instruments Shows U.S. Business How to Survive in the 1980's," *Business Week,* 18 September 1978, pp. 66–92.

7

URBAN POLITICAL LEGACIES AND CITY EXPENDITURE CONTRASTS

Young and old cities hold strikingly different competitive positions within the national economy. For the most part, their divergent economic positions reflect market outcomes, as shaped by long-term changes in technology, in resource valuations, and in consumption patterns. But it is also clear that market factors have been reinforced by governmental influences, notably including local fiscal variables. In particular, local expenditures and taxes tend to range higher in old than in young cities.

The message of this chapter is that the old city's high spending and taxes—barriers to its economic redevelopment—are a predictable consequence of its distinctive fiscal institutions, not simply the result of bad management or fiscal "irresponsibility." Hence a rejuvenation strategy, to be effective, would require provisions for city fiscal relief, measures to neutralize the institutional influences contributing to the industrial city's decline.

This argument is complicated by the technical consideration that city spending is constrained by revenue availability. During the 1970s, of course, the old cities have experienced binding revenue constraints on expenditure growth, New York City being only the most sensational example. So as to make reasonable conjectures about the un-

131

knowable true relationship governing city expenditure determination, we must therefore sort through data for two very different fiscal years: one (fiscal 1970) approximating calendar 1969, the peak of the boom, and the other covering 1975, when *cutting back* had become the highest priority for the fiscal managers of the industrial cities.

CITY–SUBURBAN CONFLICT AND LOCAL FISCAL ORGANIZATION

The upshot of Chapter 4 was that local fiscal arrangements in the United States are political variables. The old city's key fiscal institutions, for example, were forged in the late-nineteenth-century struggle between established urban elites and the New Immigrants. The consequences today are (*a*) long-frozen city boundaries (rigid city–suburban separation) and (*b*) a tradition (one dating back to the classical political machines) of city responsibility for the poor. On the other hand, most young cities are comparatively free from such legacies.

These differing modes of city–suburban interaction can be expected to create pressures for higher spending in old than in young cities. In perhaps the best definition of the suburban exploitation hypothesis, for example, Harvey Brazer has linked city expenditure levels to central-city poverty, and both to suburban exclusionary practices:

> To the extent that suburban communities, through zoning regulations and discriminatory practices in rentals and real estate transactions, contribute directly to *the concentration in the central city of socioeconomic groups which impose heavy demands upon local government services*, they are, in fact, exploiting the central city.[1]

The corollary of Brazer's definition is that old, territorially sealed cities should spend more than cities able to annex new land. The suburban exclusionary practices he describes presuppose the political containment of the central city. But that has not happened in most younger areas. On this count, there should be a commensurately diminished concentration of the poor within their central cities. If so,

---

1. Harvey E. Brazer, "Some Fiscal Implications of Metropolitanism," in *City and Suburb: The Economics of Metropolitan Growth*, ed. Benjamin Chinitz (Englewood Cliffs: Prentice-Hall, 1964), p. 144. (Emphasis added.)

then (as per Brazer's reference to service demands) some types of municipal and local spending should vary accordingly.

SOCIOSPATIAL SYSTEMS (REVISITED)

Moreover, political differences codified in state annexation laws are intensified by the divergent "sociospatial systems" of young and old cities.[2] In Chapter 4, we saw that variations in the transportation technologies available when urban areas first reached large size show up today in differing average metropolitan densities. In general, the dozen older areas retain average densities almost twice as high as those of younger areas.

Such density differences are important because they point up a spatial mechanism that contributes to poverty's differential concentration in the old city. The older urban area's higher average density reflects higher densities at its *core* than are found in the cores of younger areas. In turn, the characteristically dense, aging, and cheap housing at the core of the older area tends to act as a magnet (through its sheer quantity and availability) for the urban poor. But a comparable filtering process has not been evident in the younger area, with its newer, more dispersed housing.

The effect of systematic contrasts in city annexation power, of course, is to heighten such real structural differences between young and old cities. Annexation contrasts have meant that by 1970 the average young city covered nearly 75% of the population of its larger urban area, as compared with only 40% for the average old city. As a result, central-city contrasts in housing age and population density are doubly striking. The average old city's pre-1939 housing share, as one illustration, is 69%—well over twice the average for the young cities.

THE IMPACT OF POVERTY ON YOUNG AND OLD CITIES

Differences in the spatial structure of urban housing stocks, as reinforced by the placement of city borders, thus imply that poverty's impact should be greater in old than in young cities. We saw that, judging by an indirect measure of central-city incomes, such was in-

2. The term is coined and explained in Oliver P. Williams, *Metropolitan Political Analysis: A Social Access Approach* (New York: Free Press, 1971).

deed the case. Our measure was the ratio of average household income in a city to that in its suburban ring, taken as a unit. Whereas old
cities displayed stereotypically lower incomes than their suburbs, the
young city's average income generally matched or exceeded that of its
ring.

At this point we might note an additional and equally suggestive
indicator of poverty's differential impact. Table 7-1 lists, for selected
cities, the share of the city's total population receiving Aid to Families
with Dependent Children (AFDC). Statistics on AFDC are compiled
only for counties, but since a dozen of the 30 largest municipalities are
coextensive with counties, we can compare their shares.

Here also, as the table reveals, a clear contrast emerges as between
young and old cities. For the young city–counties, AFDC counts taken
in early 1977 fell near or below the national average. But they reached
far higher proportions in the industrial cities of the Manufacturing
Belt. The proportions in New York (11%) and Boston (14%) were
more than double the national average. But the proportions climbed

TABLE 7-1

Recipients of Aid to Families with Dependent Children in Large City – Counties,
February 1977

City, by AFDC share	Number in February 1977	Percentage of estimated 1975 city population
St. Louis	86,000[a]	16.4
Baltimore	133,000	15.7
Philadelphia	269,000	14.8
Boston	99,000	13.7
Washington	95,000	13.4
New York	844,000	11.3
New Orleans	61,000	11.0
San Francisco	50,000	7.6
Denver	35,000	7.3
U.S. average	—	5.3
Indianapolis	40,000	5.1
Jacksonville	26,000	4.7
Nashville	19,000	4.4

Source: U.S. Department of Health, Education, and Welfare, Social Security Administration, *Public Assistance Recipients and Cash Payments, By Program, State, and County, February 1977* (Washington, D.C.: U.S. Department of Health, Education, and Welfare, August 1977).

[a] Numbers are rounded to the nearest thousand.

even higher in Philadelphia, Baltimore, and St. Louis, where one on six of the city's residents received AFDC payments.

THE STRUCTURE OF EXPENDITURE VARIATIONS IN FISCAL 1970

Whatever the indicator, the results are in line with the notion of differentially concentrated poverty in the old cities. So our hypothesis is clearly defined. As repositories for the urban poor, old cities can be expected to display higher local expenditure levels than the central cities of younger, less spatially polarized urban areas.

With that as background, the obvious next step is to check the actual pattern of city and local government spending for 1970. Accordingly, Table 7-2 presents three different versions of the expenditure variable. Each depicts a different measure of city or local per capita spending within the borders of the 30 largest cities in fiscal 1970. The first item is per capita city government spending for current or operating expenditures. Omitted from this series are city outlays for irregularly budgeted projects like the construction of a bridge or hospital.

The second column does include such capital expenses. It lists total municipal spending per capita. But Column 2 still renders an incomplete picture of local expenditures within city borders, because it omits the expenditures of the school districts, county governments, and special districts that may also provide services to city residents. The last column fills in this gap; it lists the combined per capita spending of both city and noncity local governments.

CONTRASTS IN SPENDING BY CITY AGE-CLASS

Regardless of the yardstick we use, spending in the old cities ranged higher than in the young ones. This age-class contrast shows up clearly in the means and differences at the bottom of the table. Whether the index is current or total city government spending, the industrial-city average was more than twice that of the young cities.

At first glance, the clarity of the contrast seems to fade for total local spending (Column 3). This series, including as it does school expenditures, begins from a higher base for each city—a base that softens the relative difference between age-class means. But because intraclass

TABLE 7-2
City and Local Per Capita Spending in the 30 Largest Cities, Fiscal 1970

Age class	City, by 1910 metropolitan size	Current general spending: municipal ($)	Total general spending: municipal ($)	Total local spending within the city ($)
Industrial	New York	754	838	894
	Chicago	163	205	478
	Philadelphia	229	299	495
	Boston	481	554	531
	Pittsburgh	154	192	450
	St. Louis	204	225	463
	San Francisco	521	603	768
	Baltimore	529	639	638
	Cleveland	159	198	512
	Buffalo	321	367	528
	Detroit	198	234	471
	Cincinnati	359	502	761
Anomalous	Los Angeles	126	169	624
	Washington	851	1011	1006
	Milwaukee	148	219	562
	Kansas City	143	245	485
	New Orleans	144	182	334
	Seattle	152	209	524
Young	Indianapolis	86	127	355
	Atlanta	158	236	554
	Denver	238	306	502
	Columbus	123	192	398
	Memphis	256	294	370
	Nashville	288	360	378
	Dallas	95	158	352
	San Antonio	64	88	252
	Houston	81	112	305
	Jacksonville	118	135	307
	San Diego	106	137	484
	Phoenix	99	130	375
Means and significance of mean differences				
Industrial cities		339	405	582
Young cities		145	190	386
Difference		194	215	196
Significance		$p < .01$	$p < .01$	$p < .001$

Source: U.S. Bureau of the Census, *City Government Finances in 1969–70* and *Local Government Finances in Selected Metropolitan Areas in 1969–70* (Washington, D.C.: Government Printing Office, 1972).

variability also falls, the arithmetic difference between age-class means is associated with an even smaller probability value than before. Classification by city age, in other words, has just as much utility for total local as for city government spending.

Still, there was so much intraclass variability that the averages were poor guides to how spending would behave in any particular city. This was especially so for the industrial cities. In terms of current city government spending, for example, the standard deviation for the old cities was $184 per capita. So whatever it was that created the contrasts between the two age classes also left room for tremendous differences among the industrial cities themselves.

Municipal Assignment Variations

The table itself provides a clue to what caused such large differences. Checking city against local spending (Columns 2 and 3), we find that city governments racked up a much higher share of the total in some cities than in others. New York, Baltimore, and Boston, for example, accounted for virtually all the local spending within their borders, whereas cities like San Antonio, San Diego, and Cleveland registered far smaller shares.

The reason for varying municipal shares, of course, is that some city governments perform more local services than others. The connection is documented in Table 7-3, which also ranks the 30 cities in order of their current municipal spending.

The table discloses an extremely powerful explanation of contrasts in spending. Its key feature is the connection between current spending and *the number of major optional programs a city performs*. (In the table, the range is from zero to three, reflecting possible combinations among schools, welfare, and colleges—each of which is administered by a few municipal governments, but not by most.) Municipal spending increases directly with that number. The more major program options, the higher a city government's per capita expenditures. For the fiscal year 1970, there were no exceptions.

This suggests that one reason for age-related contrasts in spending is that the governments of the industrial cities were more likely to perform the really expensive optional programs.[3] At the same time,

3. During fiscal 1970, New York and Washington administered all three major optional programs—schools, welfare, and a system of higher education. Baltimore ad-

TABLE 7-3

Municipal Fiscal Scale and Per Capita Current City Expenditures in the 30 Largest Cities, Fiscal 1970

City, by amount spent per capita	Current per capita municipal general expenditure	No. of major "optional" city services (schools, colleges, welfare)	City's percentage share of total local spending
Washington	851	3	100
New York	754	3	94
Baltimore	529	2	100
San Francisco	521	1	79
Boston	481	1	104
Cincinnati	359	1	66
Buffalo	321	1	70
Nashville	288	1	95
Memphis	256	1	79
Denver	238	1	61
Philadelphia	229	0	60
St. Louis	204	0	49
Detroit	198	0	50
Chicago	163	0	43
Cleveland	159	0	39
Atlanta	158	0	43
Pittsburgh	154	0	43
Seattle	152	0	40
Milwaukee	148	0	39
New Orleans	144	0	54
Kansas City	143	0	51
Los Angeles	126	0	27
Columbus	123	0	48
Jacksonville	118	0	44
San Diego	106	0	28
Phoenix	99	0	35
Dallas	95	0	45
Indianapolis	86	0	36
Houston	81	0	37
San Antonio	64	0	35

Source: Same as for Table 7-2.

however, the correspondence between city age and municipal program assignment was only an approximate one. Moreover, it is obvious from Table 7-3 that cities carrying the same number of big optional programs spent widely varying amounts. In short, a good deal remains to be explained.

The key to this "residual variation" is that *among municipal governments with comparable program loads, the ones for the industrial cities spent more.* Of the half-dozen cities performing a single major optional program, for example, the old cities spent larger amounts than the rest. Or again, from among the majority of city governments that were free from responsibility for any of the three options, the governments of the old cities of Philadelphia, St. Louis, and Detroit spent three times as much as some of the governments of the young cities. Just as assignment variations cut across age categories, in other words, so also was the tendency toward higher old-city spending more than a matter of program loads alone.

And that brings us back to the question of the differing political legacies of young and old cities. It has been suggested that a central city's territorial range should influence its per capita expenditures. The old city's frozen borders, its ancient core housing and social infrastructure, and above all its concentrated poverty might all reasonably be expected to raise average service costs and to increase demands for city services. Conversely, the dispersed young city, covering a broader assortment of the urban population, should benefit from more favorable service conditions and from a diminished demand for poverty-related services.

LOCAL FISCAL INSTITUTIONS AS THE "DETERMINANTS" OF CITY EXPENDITURES

So we have two administrative outcomes—municipal program assignment and city territorial coverage—that might explain the ten-

---

ministered schools and welfare. Among the cities handling one major option, Cincinnati administered higher education; Boston, Buffalo, Memphis, and Nashville, school systems; and Denver and San Francisco, welfare. As will be seen in a later section (pages 152–153), fiscal assignments can change. During the 1970s, for example, following its consolidation with Marion County, the city government of Indianapolis has picked up a welfare assignment.

dency toward higher spending in old cities. When per capita current spending is regressed on the two variables, the results are as follows:

$$S_i = 250 - 2.0B_i + 209P_{1i} + 392P_{2i} + 631P_{3i}, \qquad (1)$$
$$ (9.5) \quad (4.7) \quad (9.7) \qquad (7.8) \qquad (17.1)$$
$$N = 30, \qquad SE = 48.8, \qquad R^2 = .95,$$

where the parenthesized terms beneath the coefficient estimates give the absolute values of the ratios of the estimates to their standard errors (the t-ratios).

The explanatory variables thus account for 95% of the variation in 1970 city government spending. To be more precise, the program dummies (P_1, P_2, and P_3) account for fully 90% by themselves. Then city territorial coverage (B, the percentage share of 1970 urbanized-area population contained within the central city's borders) manages to explain half the remaining variation.

A word about the program dummies: P_1, P_2, and P_3. According to Eq. (1), a city administering one major optional program spent an additional $209 per capita, whereas a city with two was fitted out as spending an additional $392.[4] Similarly, a city government performing all three programs—schools, welfare, and a university—is estimated to have spent an additional $631. In all three cases, the statistical estimates carry unusually high t-ratios.[5]

THE INTERPLAY BETWEEN BORDERS AND FISCAL ASSIGNMENT

The equation also indicates a statistically powerful relationship between a city's territorial coverage and expenditure levels. On average, each additional percentage point of the urban population a city in-

---

4. The estimated coefficients are thus mutually exclusive, *not* additive.

5. It might be noted that very few of the dozens of determinants studies have specified differences in administrative assignments. Perhaps the best known determinants studies, for example, are Amos W. Hawley, "Metropolitan Population and Municipal Expenditures in Central Cities," *Journal of Social Issues*, 7 (1951), pp. 100–108; Harvey E. Brazer, *City Expenditures in the United States* (New York: National Bureau of Economic Research, 1959); and Roy W. Bahl, *Metropolitan City Expenditures: A Comparative Analysis* (Lexington: University of Kentucky Press, 1969). None of the three tested variables for municipal or local fiscal assignment. The cost of that omission is that any variables which are tested and are correlated with assignment (e.g., population density, a consensus selection as a key "determinant," and a variable ranging higher in old than in young cities) will be fitted with systematically biased estimates. The other cost, of course, is that the really large differences in spending will remain unexplained.

cludes is associated with a decrease of $2 per capita. By this estimate, the predicted difference between, say, St. Louis and San Antonio (one old, one young, with similar program assignments) is $104 per capita, or $2 multiplied by the 52-point difference in territorial coverage.

Figure 7-1 depicts the interplay between program assignment and a city's territorial coverage. In terms of the example just given, St. Louis and San Antonio both lie near the bottom regression line, reflecting the fact that neither administers any of the three big optional programs. But because it covers only 33% of the urban population, St. Louis is fitted far to the left and thus has a substantially higher predicted value.

In sum, the two institutional variables yield a successful description of the array of municipal spending differences in 1970—and of the tendency for expenditures to range higher in old than in young cities. In a less technical format, Fred Hofheinz, while mayor of Houston, offered a strikingly similar explanation: "In Houston and other Texas cities we are willing to spend property taxes for city services, but only for basic city services like fire and police protection, streets and sewers. Not for higher education. Not for welfare matching. Not for a wide range of social service functions that many other cities [do]."[6] Hofheinz's interpretation differs from ours only in that he seems to suggest that "optional" city programs like welfare are literally optional, rather than state-assigned.

Nor does his characterization refer to program assignment alone. As he adds in a slightly different context, "We have our blight, we have our areas of decay. But because of the annexation, our problems get lost in the average." In terms of Eq. (1), of course, this comment suggests why a city's per capita spending should fall as the city's territorial coverage (B) increases.

But there is one issue Hofheinz raises, which we have yet to pin down. To what extent do municipal (or, for that matter, total local) spending differences result in higher *taxes?* This is a complicated question. As will be seen shortly, in some circumstances it may be more realistic to reverse the approach, viewing tax revenues as a binding constraint on spending. In addition, state aid for optional services varies widely. Still, Eq. (2) reveals that per capita taxes varied predictably with the two institutional determinants:

6. Quotations appear in Jonathan Wolman, "Houston vs. Detroit: 'greedy vs. the needy?'" *Dallas Times-Herald,* 9 December 1976.

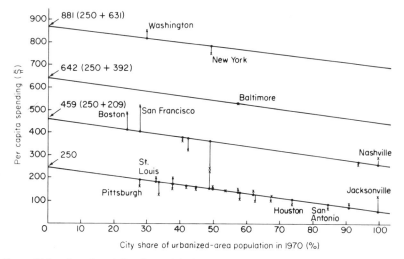

Figure 7-1. Actual and fitted municipal current expenditures per capita for the 30 largest cities in fiscal 1970.

$$T_i = 189 - 1.5B_i + 78P_{1i} + 121P_{2i} + 322P_{3i}, \qquad (2)$$
$$\quad (7.0) \quad (3.6) \quad (3.6) \quad (2.4) \quad (8.6)$$
$$N = 30, \qquad SE = 49.7, \qquad R^2 = .82.$$

COMBINED LOCAL SPENDING AND TAXES IN FISCAL 1970

Similar results may be obtained for aggregate local expenditures and taxes. Turning from municipal to combined local variables does, however, require changes in the program dummies. In particular, the number of major optional programs can now be reduced from three to two. Since some local unit is going to finance schools within every city's borders, we can ignore schools as a cause of spending contrasts. So now the dummies will indicate whether welfare and higher education are administered by any local government (including counties as well as city governments). Now Los Angeles, for example, will be specified as having one major option, since Los Angeles County administers (and imposes taxes for) public assistance within the city.

Again, the results are good:

$$LS_i = 632 - 3.6B_i + 129LP_{1i} + 459LP_{2i}, \qquad (3)$$
$$\quad (16.3) \quad (5.9) \quad (4.6) \quad (8.6)$$
$$N = 30, \qquad SE = 68.9, \qquad R^2 = .86.$$

Now, with school spending added in, the constant rises to more than $600 per capita. From this amount, local spending falls by $3.60 for each 1% of the urban population included within city borders. The effect of one big extra program is $129 in additional spending; of two, $459 per capita. All estimates are significant at probability values of .01.

When combined local taxes are regressed on these same variables, the results hold up remarkably well—almost as well as for municipal taxes alone. Despite variations in state aid for welfare and higher education, local taxes can be seen to vary systematically with our institutional variables. Taxes rise an estimated $2.60 per capita for each 1-point reduction in a city's relative territorial coverage. They also increase, as expected, with each additional program:

$$LT_i = 368 - 2.6B_i + 38LP_{1i} + 183LP_{2i}, \qquad (4)$$
$$(15.3) \quad (6.9) \quad (2.2) \quad (5.6)$$
$$N = 30, \qquad SE = 42.7, \qquad R^2 = .80.$$

THE REVENUE CONSTRAINT AND THE 1976 RANKINGS

So far, so good. Our two institutional variables explain all but a slight fraction of municipal and local spending differences for fiscal 1970. The first (and the source of the really large expenditure contrasts) is city or local program assignment. With some variation, the governments of the old cites tend to carry heavier program loads, and, thus, to outspend young cities by large amounts. The second is city territorial coverage, as shaped by state annexation guidelines. Whereas program loads give rise to quantum differences among cities, the borders variable generates incremental expenditure variations.[7] For cities characterized by similar program loads, then, spending ranged higher in the tightly bounded old cities, whose borders contain massive poverty.

Taxes varied accordingly, which suggests that local fiscal institutions do indeed create locational incentives favoring young cities.

7. Not only because of higher service demands, but because of *cost* differentials as well. A useful account of the role of service conditions in the production functions for local services is D. F. Bradford, R. A. Malt, and W. E. Oates, "The Rising Cost of Local Public Services: Some Evidence and Reflections," *National Tax Journal*, 22 (June 1969), pp. 185–202.

State aid variations introduce an added element of uncertainty to the relationship, of course. But despite such variations, city and local taxes varied predictably with the two institutional variables.

The obvious question is, how have these relationships held up during the 1970s? And a more subtle issue also needs attention. In view of their stagnant economies, how can declining old cities continue to *finance* their higher per capita spending? The answers to these questions will reveal the strategic significance of federal fiscal relief.

MUNICIPAL DETERMINANTS REGRESSIONS FOR FISCAL 1976

Judging by updated determinants regressions, a robust relationship links city fiscal outcomes and local administrative structures. When city government spending for fiscal 1976 is regressed on the two determinants, the results remain impressive:

$$S_i = 572 - 4.9B_i + 363P_{1i} + 619P_{2i} + 1370P_{3i}, \qquad (5)$$
$$(10.5) \ (5.5) \quad (8.4) \qquad (5.9) \qquad (17.7)$$
$$N = 30, \qquad SE = 102.7, \qquad R^2 = .94.$$

If anything, the municipal tax regression performs better for fiscal 1976 than for fiscal 1970. In particular, its explanatory power, as measured by the R^2, has risen by several percentage points:

$$T_i = 310 - 2.6B_i + 121P_{1i} + 152P_{2i} + 619P_{3i}, \qquad (6)$$
$$(8.1) \ (4.1) \quad (4.0) \qquad (2.0) \qquad (11.3)$$
$$N = 30, \qquad SE = 72.3, \qquad R^2 = .87.$$

As we would expect, given the rapid pace of inflation between 1969 and 1975, the coefficients for both equations are dramatically higher than they were before. Otherwise, not much has changed.

FISCAL MANAGEMENT AND THE REVENUE CONSTRAINT

From the standpoint of revenue availability, it is surprising that the equations should hold up so well over time. Fiscal 1976 includes most of calendar 1975, a year of severe recession, and, hence, of forced budgetary cutbacks. (By contrast, of course, fiscal 1970 overlapped with 1969, a boom year, when municipal coffers were comparatively full.) Most industrial cities were hit harder by the recession than most young ones. One might therefore expect some of the initially higher-spending old cities to have cut their spending growth sharply below that of the young cities.

Putting it more formally, the revenue constraint should have cut more deeply into the old cities' expenditure functions.[8] Unlike the federal government, state and local governments are typically proscribed from borrowing long-term to pay for current expenses. As a result, the productivity of the local tax base and the availability of intergovernmental aid directly constrain the amounts city and other local governments can spend without raising taxes. For a given aid package and a given set of tax rates, current spending is thus limited by the productivity of the tax base.[9]

Age-Class Contrasts for 1976

As it happens, per capita spending did tend to rise less rapidly in old than in young cities between fiscal 1970 and fiscal 1976. Considering the fiscal horror stories emanating from Boston, Detroit, and other old cities besides New York, that comes as no surprise. Their revenue capacity has grown slowly, if at all. Meanwhile, Dallas, Phoenix, and most other young cities have been able to draw on expanding tax bases to finance expenditure growth without raising tax rates.

Yet this slower expenditure growth in the old cities had little real impact on the 1976 age-class contrasts. As Table 7-4 shows, the governments of the old cities again averaged over twice as much per capita as those of the young cities. For current spending, the figures are $681 versus $308 (and for total spending, which is not listed, $806 versus $406). But from the standpoint of the larger argument,

8. For an invaluable survey of this and other econometric issues concerning the specification of determinants equations, see Jesse Burkhead and Jerry Miner, *Public Expenditures* (Chicago: Aldine, 1970), chapter 9.

9. The revenue constraint's influence on a cross-section of city governments during a given year was documented by Scott and Feder during the 1950s. Their study described spending variations for cities within a single state, where service assignments varied less than among cities nationally. They concluded that the principal explanation for spending differences among California cities was per-capita tax base disparities—that is, differences in revenue availability. See Stanley Scott and Edward L. Feder, *Factors Associated with the Variations in Municipal Expenditure Levels* (Berkeley: University of California, 1957).

TABLE 7-4
Municipal Spending and Taxes Per Capita in Fiscal 1976

Age class	City, by 1910 metropolitan size	Current municipal general spending ($)	Municipal taxes ($)
Industrial	New York	1625	743
	Chicago	306	201
	Philadelphia	482	257
	Boston	1024	516
	Pittsburgh	256	138
	St. Louis	426	281
	San Francisco	850	459
	Baltimore	911	315
	Cleveland	348	149
	Buffalo	678	233
	Detroit	418	227
	Cincinnati	843	226
Anomalous	Los Angeles	282	196
	Washington	1879	912
	Milwaukee	267	118
	Kansas City	354	244
	New Orleans	337	161
	Seattle	345	166
Young	Indianapolis	307	121
	Atlanta	344	189
	Denver	577	261
	Columbus	256	123
	Memphis	402	115
	Nashville	498	314
	Dallas	220	191
	San Antonio	161	72
	Houston	196	158
	Jacksonville	300	108
	San Diego	212	113
	Phoenix	227	111
	Class means		
Industrial cities		681	312
Young cities		308	156
Difference		373	156
Significance		$p < .01$	(Not computed.)

Source: U.S. Bureau of the Census, *City Government Finances in 1975–76* (Washington, D.C.: U.S. Government Printing Office, 1977).

perhaps the key point concerns municipal taxes per capita. In fiscal 1976, *city taxes averaged $312 for the old cities, exactly double the young-city average.*

Varieties of Fiscal Response to Decline

City-by-city, the 1976 array does suggest that the governments of the old cities are responding to decline in fiscally diverse ways. At one end of the spectrum are Chicago and Pittsburgh, traditionally tightly managed cities whose response has been to hold a close rein on expenditure growth. As Table 7-5 and Figure 7-2 reveal, their governments spent less in fiscal 1976 than did comparably burdened governments of some young cities. On the other hand, by 1976 such old cities as Detroit, St. Louis, and Philadelphia were outspending young-city governments with *heavier* program loads. On balance, the rule still holds: Where program loads are similar, most old cities outspend most young ones. But now this simple rank ordering is losing some of its earlier clarity. These diverse fiscal responses to stagnant or even shrinking city tax bases point up a key issue for urban policy design. Given the perversity of local fiscal institutions, can the old city's officials "manage" decline without driving away more of the tax base?

THE LOGIC OF FEDERAL FISCAL RELIEF TO DECLINING CITIES

This chapter's guiding hypothesis has been that the industrial city's political legacy has accelerated its economic decline. As Chapter 4 suggested, the old city's key fiscal institutions were forged before World War I, in the contest for social control of spatial access. The results today are immutable city boundaries and a tradition of central-city responsibility for the urban poor. Both legacies generate pressures for higher expenditures—and, therefore, taxes—in old than in young cities. Old cities have differentially concentrated poverty, contained within tightly binding borders, and their governments are more likely to administer the big optional programs. Young cities have generally lighter program loads. They also have diversified populations and territorially inclusive boundaries—each of which

TABLE 7-5

Fiscal Scale and Per Capita Current City Expenditures in Fiscal 1976

City, by amount spent per capita	Current per capita municipal general expenditure ($)	No. of major "optional" city services (schools, colleges, welfare)
Washington	1879	3
New York	1625	3
Boston	1024	1
Baltimore	911	2
San Francisco	850	1
Cincinnati	843	1
Buffalo	678	1
Denver	577	1
Nashville	498	1
Philadelphia	482	0
St. Louis	426	0
Detroit	418	0
Memphis	402	1
Kansas City	354	0
Cleveland	348	0
Seattle	345	0
Atlanta	344	0
New Orleans	337	0
Indianapolis	307	1
Chicago	306	0
Jacksonville	300	0
Los Angeles	282	0
Milwaukee	267	0
Pittsburgh	256	0
Columbus	256	0
Phoenix	227	0
Dallas	220	0
San Diego	212	0
Houston	196	0
San Antonio	161	0

Source: Same as for Table 7-4.

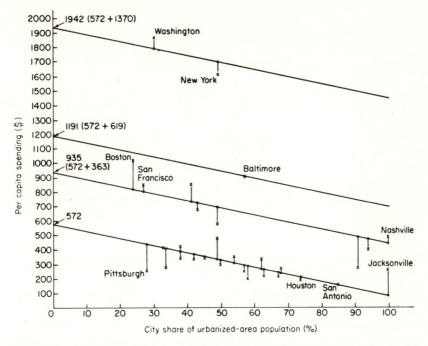

Figure 7-2. Actual and fitted municipal current expenditures per capita for the 30 largest cities in fiscal 1976.

tends to diminish effective service demands and reduce service costs.[10]

Fiscal legacies thus pose serious obstacles to a rejuvenation strategy. The old city's high taxes and redistributive services constitute an obvious barrier to any system of private incentives for its redevelopment. Hence a rejuvenation plan should include provisions for fiscal relief—measures to neutralize the fiscal influences contributing to the old city's decline.

10. Earlier studies have found that spending ranges higher in declining than in growing cities. (See the Bahl study cited in Note 5, for example, or Thomas Muller, "The Declining and Growing Metropolis—A Fiscal Comparison," in *Post-Industrial America: Metropolitan Decline and Inter-Regional Job Shifts,* eds. George Sternlieb and James W. Hughes, New Brunswick, Center for Urban Policy Research, 1975, pp. 197–220.) The evidence appraised in this chapter suggests that a more accurate depiction would be to say that fiscal magnitudes vary as between old cities (which are declining) and young cities (which are not). The reason? Fiscal *institutions* differ as between old and young cities in ways that generate the observed pattern of expenditure differences.

FISCAL OPTIONS

Even if not linked to a rejuvenation plan, of course, neutralizing the old city's perverse fiscal legacy is a plausible goal for federal policy. The question is how it might be pursued. One approach to this question is to consider the standard menu of choices said to be available to fiscally strapped city governments.[11] The list can be reappraised in light of the chapter's institutional model of fiscal determinants. Our purpose will be to select policy measures that are (*a*) benign in their effects on a city's economic position and (*b*) politically feasible.

A fiscally distressed city government can (1) borrow to pay for current expenses, (2) increase city taxes, or (3) cut expenditures. It can also press for changes in institutional arrangements. In line with our model, the key institutional reforms sometimes suggested are (4) metropolitan government and the (5) transfer of municipal or other local programs to state or federal governments. An alternative to such large-scale changes is (6) increased aid from a higher government.

To repeat, each of these possibilities can be appraised briefly in terms of its economic neutrality and political feasibility. As is summarized in Table 7-6, the first three have adverse effects on the city's economy. But the remaining three, requiring as they do action by a higher government, are politically uncertain.

THE INSTITUTIONAL ALTERNATIVES TO RETRENCHMENT

Borrowing to Cover Current Spending

Recurrent fiscal strain provides a powerful inducement for city officials to try to supplement current revenues via borrowing. As noted earlier, the statutes of most states rule out such behavior. So juggling the books to make current expenses look like capital items (which *can* be loan-financed) may prove tempting. As the New York episode revealed, this sort of maneuvering can be disastrous— politically and economically. Left to their own devices, fiscal managers in a declining city must therefore either raise taxes or cut spending.

City Tax Increases

While the old city's per capita tax base grows slowly if at all, unit service costs, afflicted by Baumol's disease, continue to rise. If service

11. As, for example, in Robert B. Pettengill and Jogindar S. Uppal, *Can Cities Survive: The Fiscal Plight of American Cities* (New York: St. Martin's Press, 1974), chapter 5.

TABLE 7-6
Fiscal Options for Declining Cities[a]

Action	Economic impact on declining city	Political feasibility
1. "Temporary" borrowing	−	−
2. Tax increases	−	+
3. Service cutbacks	−	+
4. Metro government	+	−
5. Program transfers	+	?
6. Aid increases		
(a) State	+	−
(b) Federal	+	+

Source: Subjective evaluations, as explained in the text.
[a] − = Negative; + = neutral or positive.

levels are to be maintained, more tax revenue is required. Since tax revenue equals the base times the rate, the only way to raise new revenue from a given base is to increase tax rates (or use new tax sources).

Tax rate increases are all but certain to aggravate a city's decline. To cite the example of a smaller old city, Newark's property tax rates of some 10% of true market value show how far the cycle can go once the contraction of the city tax base begins. They also assure that no private-sector redevelopment will ever take place spontaneously in that city. While Newark may be the limiting case, the cycle it illustrates is common to the industrial cities.

Service Cutbacks

As an alternative to tax increases, the government of a declining city can cut services. Service cutbacks seem politically more respectable to outside observers than city tax increases. But like tax hikes, cutbacks place the city at a competitive disadvantage. (Poverty-related services may constitute an exception, since the poor may have no superior locational alternatives.) To believe that cutbacks can be neutral for non-poverty services is to assume that the city's services were not demanded by taxpayers in the first place. If not, why were the provided?

The upshot is that the task of fiscal management in a declining city is retrenchment. But retrenchment, however pursued, hurts a city's competitive position relative either to its suburbs or to the young cities. *The only resolution of this fiscal dilemma is institutional change.* In its absence, sound fiscal management will have the paradoxical effect of driving the old city's economy down.

Metropolitan Government

One such institutional change, long advocated as a means for cities to outflank the suburbanization of the tax base, is metropolitan or areawide government. In a gradual shift of opinion, "metro" government is increasingly viewed by scholars as not only politically unattainable, but as inefficient. Be that as it may, the irony is that from Toronto to Indianapolis to Jacksonville, from London to Houston or Oklahoma City to Phoenix, reasonable approximations to metropolitan government are everywhere. Whatever its impact on economic welfare, there can be no real doubt about the approach's workability.

The question is not whether metro government could ever work in practice, but only whether it is a realistic prospect for the industrial city. Only in the deadlocked industrial metropolis, in other words, could such a widely used system seem a utopian vision. And yet that is precisely what it does seem: not politically feasible.

Poverty-Related Program Transfers

The old city's legacy of responsibility for the urban poor influences city spending and taxes through specific and demonstrable program assignments. Not much has been said on the linkages between poverty, program assignments, and city taxes, but that omission can be remedied easily here. As a background point, only welfare and higher education need to be considered. Unlike local schools, both imply net additions to the tax bills city residents pay—and both are directly related to poverty.[12]

For perspective on the link between the two major poverty assignments and city age, it helps to go back a few years, say to 1960. In that year, there were seven instances of young or old cities performing either or both of the poverty services. Six of these seven were old. In other words, *half the industrial cities then carried either welfare or higher-*

---

12. Though state aid practices can reduce the local taxes required. In Baltimore, for example, the city-administered welfare program is financed almost entirely through federal and state grants. By contrast, New York City finances about 25% of its huge welfare bill from its own tax revenue.

education assignments. By contrast, from the 18 remaining old and young cities, only two administered either program.

The correlation is no longer so evident, because program assignments, immutable though they seem, can be altered. In key institutional changes during the 1960s, Massachusetts and Michigan relieved Boston and Detroit of the public-assistance assignment. But considering the historical tension between the industrial cities and their state governments, it is difficult to foresee the likelihood of further major transfers. What is clear, from the standpoint of the old cities' economic positions, is their desirability.

Federal Fiscal Relief

All of which leaves increased aid as perhaps the only option that is both economically benign and politically feasible. Or is it feasible? Unrestricted state aid to cities has not shown any notable increase since 1950, and there is no obvious reason to expect that to change. What has changed dramatically during the 1970s is *federal* fiscal relief—the key factor enabling numerous declining cities to avoid even more severe cutbacks. The rationale for such aid is considered in the next chapter.

8

URBAN DIFFERENCES AND FEDERAL GRANT FORMULAS

In a nation of urban differences, a key issue is how federal grants to cities should be distributed. Comparably sized cities like Phoenix and Cleveland find themselves in dramatically different positions and face sharply divergent futures. Does Cleveland's economic, social, and fiscal malaise mean that it should get more help? Or are extra federal dollars to the governments of Cleveland and other declining old cities being poured into a lost cause?

Not surprisingly, questions of this kind have sparked considerable debate. In early 1978, for example, Louie Welch (Houston's former mayor and at the time president of its Chamber of Commerce) announced a new research group to defend the interests of the South and West as against those of the heartland. As the basis for his call to battle, he gave a seemingly clear statement of the new group's purpose. "All we want," he said, "is a national urban policy that's fair."

But Welch's remarks were not really aimed at the new Carter urban policy. His complaint had a more specific focus:

During the last two years, it has become apparent that a relative handful of states has been draining off a disproportionately high share of federal grant dollars because federal program dollars are being awarded on the basis of *discriminatory formulas tilted to the advantage of certain regions* and to the detriment of others.[1]

The grant formulas in question favor declining old cities. One might assume, of course, that city officials and their representatives will press for maximum federal money for their particular bailiwicks. But how should the rest of us view "discriminatory formulas," grant formulas that target limited federal funds to localities deemed to have special needs?

The purpose of the chapter is to explore this question. The chapter reviews the evolution of the formula Welch condemns (one used to distribute Community Development Block Grants). We will find that the issue may be less what is *fair* in the abstract than what is *efficient*, in relation to specified policy goals, as determined politically. At the same time, however, a case can be made that formulas favoring declining old cities serve ends most people would probably agree upon.

MEASURING CENTRAL-CITY DIFFERENCES

It will prove useful as background to consider several attempts to measure differences among cities for policy purposes. Such attempts can be grouped into two general categories. The first, the taxonomy, is illustrated by the age classification used in this book. The second type attempts to develop more fine-grained measures, quantitative indexes that can be used for practical purposes.

RELATIVE BIG-CITY POSITIONS: THREE TAXONOMIES

Our age-classification scheme is premised on the idea that a city's broad economic and political circumstances today depend on the timing of its formative development. As was outlined in Chapter 2, the informal hypothesis guiding this study is that a city's age shapes its (*a*) economic performance since 1945, (*b*) political isolation or integration within its larger urban area, and (*c*) key fiscal institutions. In turn, both city fiscal distress and the urban problem in general have been traced to the telltale economic and political legacies of the industrial

1. Quoted in *Dallas Times-Herald*, 31 March 1978. (Emphasis added.)

cities as a class. This system can be compared with two other recently fashioned big-city taxonomies, one covering not the 30 but the 40 largest cities, the other, the central cities of 67 large SMSAs.

The first, which is based largely on subjective impressions, yields a list of problem cities dominated by our industrial cities.[2] These are listed in Table 8-1 as "declining and vulnerable" cities, a designation that differentiates them from cities that have lost population during the 1970s, but are viewed as basically healthy. Most of our young cities fall into a different category still: cities that are simply growing.

The second uses objective, short-term criteria to classify 67 of the 75 largest cities. Prepared for the Joint Economic Committee, it groups cities according to (a) whether they gained or lost population between 1970 and 1975 and (b) whether their unemployment rates in 1976 were above or below the U.S. average.[3] Of the 11 industrial cities considered, 10 appear in the group listed as hurting on both counts (Table 8-2). By contrast, only two of the young cities (Atlanta and Denver) are in this camp. Considering the short-term (and thus, perhaps, volatile) character of the two criteria, the correspondence seems reasonably close.

INDEXING CITY "HARDSHIP"

In any case, none of the three taxonomies provides a standard that is inclusive and discriminating enough to aid policy design. For that purpose attempts have been made to develop general indicators of city need or "hardship." An interesting initial foray in this direction is a collection of multivariate classification schemes, *City Classification Handbook,* which appeared in the early 1970s.[4] As its editor concluded, however, none of the factor-analytic scoring systems used in the book seem adequate to practical tasks of policy implementation. As later efforts would demonstrate, this caveat was fundamental. To economists in particular, factor scores will seem inherently ill-defined as indicators of specific urban conditions or needs.

2. John Craig and Michael Koleda, "The Future of the Municipal Hospital in Major American Cities" (processed, April 1976).

3. U.S. Congress, Joint Economic Committee, *The Current Fiscal Condition of Cities: A Survey of 67 of the 75 Largest Cities,* as cited in Committee for Economic Development, *An Approach to Federal Urban Policy* (New York: 1977), p. 39.

4. Edited by Brian J. L. Berry (New York: Wiley, 1972).

TABLE 8-1
The Relative "Vulnerability" of the 40 Largest Cities: A Subjective Taxonomy

Declining and vulnerable cities	Declining but basically healthy cities	Growing cities
New York	Los Angeles	Houston
Chicago	Washington	Dallas
Philadelphia	Indianapolis	San Diego
Detroit	Milwaukee	San Antonio
Baltimore	San Francisco	Memphis
Cleveland	Boston	Phoenix
St. Louis	New Orleans	Columbus
Pittsburgh	Seattle	Atlanta
Buffalo	Jacksonville	Fort Worth
Cincinnati	Denver	San Jose
Newark	Kansas City	Oklahoma City
	Minneapolis	Nashville
	Toledo	
	Portland	
	Oakland	
	Louisville	
	Long Beach	

Source: Same as for Table 2-3.

The Brookings Hardship Index

A simpler and widely influential system of scoring cities is the Brookings hardship index designed by Richard Nathan and Charles Adams.[5] Based on 1970 data for the central cities of 55 of the 66 largest SMSAs, the index is an average of standardized values for six socioeconomic variables: unemployment, dependency (i.e., the share of a city's population under 18 or over 65), education, real per capita income, crowded housing, and poverty. For each of the six, values were expressed in terms of a range from 0 for the lowest observation, 100 for the highest. A city's score was then defined as its average value for the six standardized variables. Of the 55 cities, Newark had most hardship (its average was 85.5) and Fort Lauderdale (with 24.0) least.

5. Richard P. Nathan and Charles Adams, "Understanding Central City Hardship," *Political Science Quarterly,* Spring 1976, pp. 47–62.

TABLE 8-2

Sixty-Seven Large Cities, Classified by 1976 Unemployment Rates and 1970–1975 Population Growth

Cities losing population, 1970–1975		Cities gaining population, 1970–1975	
With high rates of unemployment in 1976[a]	With low rates of unemployment in 1976	With high rates of unemployment in 1976	with low rates of unemployment in 1976
New York	Chicago	San Diego	Houston
Los Angeles	Dallas	Honolulu	San Antonio
Philadelphia	Indianapolis	San Jose	Phoenix
Detroit	Columbus	El Paso	Memphis
Baltimore	Kansas City	Miami	Jacksonville
Washington	Minneapolis	Tampa	Omaha
Milwaukee	Oklahoma City	Sacramento	Tulsa
San Francisco	Fort Worth	Corpus Christi	Austin
Cleveland	Louisville		Tucson
Boston	St. Paul		Baton Rouge
New Orleans	Birmingham		St. Petersburg
St. Louis	Wichita		Virginia Beach
Seattle	Richmond		Mobile
Denver	Dayton		Anaheim
Pittsburgh	Des Moines		Shreveport
Atlanta	Grand Rapids		Knoxville
Cincinnati			Fort Wayne
Toledo			Colorado Springs
Portland			
Long Beach			
Oakland			
Akron			
Jersey City			
Yonkers			
Syracuse			

Source: U.S. Congress, Joint Economic Committee, *The Current Fiscal Condition of Cities: A Survey of 67 of the 75 Largest Cities,* as cited in Committee for Economic Development, *An Approach to Federal Urban Policy* (New York: 1977).

[a] "High" and "low" unemployment rates are unemployment rates above and below the U.S. average for 1976.

In Table 8-3, the age classification is checked against the Brookings index, and against their related index of city–suburban disparities. The results are generally as one might expect, but there are two notable exceptions. By either the absolute or the relative (i.e., to its suburbs) index, San Francisco differs completely from the old cities of the Manufacturing Belt. On the other hand, Atlanta's scores place that city squarely among the old cities. By these socioeconomic indicators then, San Francisco acts like a young city and Atlanta like an old one. Incidentally, the city faring best by both indicators is not young, but anomalous: Seattle.

Real Income as a Basic Indicator

Lest we lose sight of the forest, we might stop to consider a single, basic indicator at this point. Some of the Brookings hardship variables are of dubious reliability. (The dependency measure varies with the placement of city borders, and the poverty variable is not adjusted for regional price-level differences.) The remaining ones could be said to boil down to a single dimension: real income, as shaped by a city's economic position, its relative territorial coverage, and the skill or educational levels of its residents.

If the purpose of a hardship index is to measure the poverty burden on a city's population, real per capita income is probably as good as any other indicator. (It is, of course, one of the six variables that went into the hardship index—but only one.) And here the data tell a strikingly clear-cut story. Table 8-4 lists per capita income, adjusted for cost-of-living differences, in the 23 largest cities for which price-level data are available.

The table shows that in 1974 (or before the 1975 recession's impact), the old cities of the heartland had uniformly lower real incomes than other large cities. Moreover, the disparities tended to be surprisingly wide. Most young cities listed had per capita real incomes of $5000 or more. But the industrial cities other than San Francisco had an average of about $4200. In its extreme form, as between Denver or Dallas at the top and Buffalo or Boston at the bottom of the scale, the contrast can only be described as stark.

THE ISSUE: CITY GOVERNMENTS OR CITY RESIDENTS?

So, real income provides a key indicator of a city population's economic position, and one that supports the life-cycle view of the urban

TABLE 8-3
City Hardship and Suburban Superiority Scores by City Age-Class[a,b]

Age class	City, by 1910 metropolitan size	City hardship index	Index of suburban superiority (100=parity)
Industrial	New York	45	211
	Chicago	49	245
	Philadelphia	50	205
	Boston	46	198
	Pittsburgh	47	146
	St. Louis	76	231
	San Francisco	29	105
	Baltimore	60	256
	Cleveland	60	331
	Buffalo	57	189
	Detroit	59	210
	Cincinnati	54	148
Anomalous	Los Angeles	38	105
	Milwaukee	42	195
	Kansas City	39	152
	New Orleans	73	168
	Seattle	28	67
Young	Indianapolis	40	124
	Atlanta	50	226
	Denver	30	143
	Columbus	35	173
	Dallas	33	97
	Houston	38	93
	San Diego	33	77
	Phoenix	40	85
Class means			
Industrial cities		53	206
Young cities (8)		37	127

Source: Richard P. Nathan and Charles Adams, "Understanding Central City Hardship," *Political Science Quarterly,* Spring 1976, pp. 47–62.

[a] Based on the Brookings "hardship index."

[b] Excluding Washington, Memphis, Nashville, San Antonio, and Jacksonville, for which indexes were not compiled.

TABLE 8-4
Estimated Real Per Capita Income in 23 Large Cities, 1974

City, by size of "real" income	"Real" income ($)[a]	Intermediate budget index[b]	Per capita money income ($)
Denver	5880	95	5585
Dallas	5870	90	5285
Seattle	5740	101	5800
Houston	5680	90	5110
San Francisco	5650	106	5990
Los Angeles	5380	98	5277
San Diego	5120	98	5016
Nashville	5060	91	4606
Atlanta	4980	91	4527
Indianapolis	4890	99	4843
Kansas City	4740	97	4601
Cincinnati[c]	4700[c]	96	4517
Pittsburgh	4560	97	4426
Chicago	4550	103	4689
Detroit	4460	100	4463
Milwaukee	4460	105	4680
Baltimore	4330	100	4330
New York	4260	116	4939
Philadelphia	4200	103	4330
St. Louis	4130	97	4006
Cleveland	3850	102	3925
Buffalo	3670	107	3928
Boston	3550	117	4157

Source: Column 2: U.S. Bureau of Labor Statistics, *Handbook of Labor Statistics* (Washington, D.C.: U.S. Government Printing Office, 1976).

[a]Equals Column 3 divided by Column 2; the quotient is then multiplied by 100 and rounded to the nearest $10.

[b]Urban U.S. equals 100.

[c]Median.

problem. But what precisely does it say about central-city hardship? This is the fundamental issue for designing grant formulas. The hardship index measures the socioeconomic characteristics of a city's population. Real income is a simpler and perhaps equally efficient indicator. But neither one provides any direct information about a city government's fiscal condition. In other words, the hardship in question is that of a city's people, not necessarily of its government. The last chapter illustrated the variety of both city institutional arrangements and approaches to city fiscal management. Both factors rule out any one-to-one correspondence between socioeconomic indicators and municipal fiscal position.

Does this conclusion mean that any "discriminatory" formula will be arbitrary or unfair? Not at all. Instead, the implication is only that the formula should have some rationale more closely geared to city fiscal position.[6] The next section illustrates this point.

THE 1977 COMMUNITY DEVELOPMENT BLOCK GRANTS FORMULA AS AN INDEX OF CITY AGE

The formula Louie Welch objected to as detrimental to Sunbelt interests is one of two formulas used to determine city allocations for Community Development Block Grants (CDBGs). This section reviews the evolution of the CDBG program and shows that, intentionally or otherwise, this 1977 formula is a fairly accurate measure of city age differences. Its effect is therefore to channel more money per city resident to old than to young cities.

COMMUNITY DEVELOPMENT BLOCK GRANTS

The Housing and Community Development Act of 1974 consolidated seven categorical aid programs—including urban renewal and model cities—into a single program of block grants for community development.[7] One purpose of the change was to shift from city-by-city competitive bidding through "grantsmanship" to a system based on objective indicators of need. Local performance criteria were simplified, and elected officials (not neighborhood organizations or special-purpose agencies) were made responsible for implementation. In addition, the act explicitly posited the goal of aiding low- and moderate-income families.

Starting in 1975, the federal government channeled about $2 billion directly to some 2500 local governments, including the roughly

6. This formulation is attributable to James Howell, chief economist of the First National Bank of Boston.

7. Information in this paragraph, and indeed in this entire section, is drawn from Harold Bunce, "An Evaluation of the Community Development Block Grant Formula," *Urban Affairs Quarterly,* forthcoming.

500 cities having populations of more than 50,000. These so-called "entitlement cities" share CDBG funds with urban counties and also with nonmetropolitan local governments (the latter receiving 20% of the money available). For fiscal 1979 the Carter Administration predicts CDBG outlays of $2.8 billion—a figure that includes discretionary (i.e., non-formula-determined) Urban Development Action Grants (UDAG's) for special projects in cities that can demonstrate need. While these amounts may not sound very high, by 1980 the CDBG money going to cities will range from perhaps $20 to well over $50 per resident.

THE TWO FORMULAS

Just how much a given city gets will depend on how the city fares vis-à-vis the distribution formulas available. Originally, the entitlement cities had a choice between what is termed a *hold-harmless* option and the first, 1974 formula. As categorical grants were replaced by the new formula-derived amounts, the result would have been to cut the shares going to large central cities and (in regional terms) to the Manufacturing Belt. But under the terms of the new formula—the one introduced in the Housing and Community Development Act of 1977—that tendency has been reversed. To see how, we must look more closely at the terms just mentioned.

First, the *hold-harmless* provision offers a means by which certain exceptionally aggressive and well-organized (i.e., grant-grabbing) city governments could be protected from aid cuts with the switch from categorical to block grants. To oversimplify slightly, hold-harmless enabled a city like Boston to continue to benefit from its earlier prowess in going after federal grants by giving the city the annual average of its 1968–1978 funding. Until fiscal 1977, a city entitled to more under this scheme than under the 1974 formual would get it. Now hold-harmless is being phased out; by fiscal 1980 it will have ended completely.

Second, the *1974 formula* (i.e., the allocation formula contained in Act of 1974) is specified in terms of a locality's population size, its overcrowded housing, and its poverty population. As noted earlier, if this were the only permanent formula, phasing out hold-harmless would eventaully cut CDBG shares to central cities and to the Manufacturing Belt as a region. Harold Bunce of HUD has showed, for example, that the share going to cities of the Northeast and North-Central regions would fall from 42 to less than 23% of the total available. For that matter, even cities of the South and West would experience declining shares—the net gainers being urban counties and localities outside metropolitan areas.

But (third), the new, "*growth-lag*" formula prevents such reductions from taking place. Beginning in 1977, a city's allocation could be computed from the weighted sum of (*a*) the city's "growth-lag," (*b*) its pre-1939 housing, and (*c*) the size of its poverty population. The growth-lag indicator is computed as the "shortfall' in a city's population growth—that is, as the difference between (*a*) the gain a city would have required to match the average population growth for all entitlement cities and (*b*) its actual population change. The other two items are computed as a city's shares of the total old (pre-1939) housing and poverty within all SMSAs.

For reasons not altogether clear, HUD people describe this new version as the *dual formula*. More clear-cut is the sense in which entitlement cities will operate (after hold-harmless has been completely phased out, in fiscal 1980) under a dual-formula system. Cities will then simply receive the higher of the two amounts—the one computed from the 1974 formula, the other from the growth-lag formula (as one might prefer to call it).

THE 1980 ALLOCATIONS UNDER
THE NEW FORMULA

As Table 8-5 shows, the result of the new formula is to channel more money per capita to old then to young cities. It is true that city governments can take the higher of two amounts, that is, the ones listed, or those computed by the 1974 formula. Still, the effect of the new formula is to improve the positions of the old cities' governments dramatically. As a result of the formula's de facto measurement of city age differences, for example, Cleveland will have a 1980 allocation of $64 per capita, or more than triple the $17 the new formula allots to Phoenix.

To return to the chapter's central question, is that disparity justified? From the standpoint of the last chapter's conclusions regarding fiscal cutbacks and decline, it may be. If one posits the goal of neu-

TABLE 8-5
Per Capita 1980 CDBG Entitlements under the "Growth-Lag" Formula

Age class	City, by 1910 metropolitan size	City's 1980 per capita entitlement under the "growth-lag" formula
Industrial	New York	35
	Chicago	43
	Philadelphia	40
	Boston	43
	Pittsburgh	60
	St. Louis	72
	San Francisco	44
	Baltimore	39
	Cleveland	64
	Buffalo	62
	Detroit	50
	Cincinnati	49
Anomalous	Los Angeles	22
	Washington	37
	Milwaukee	35
	Kansas City	28
	New Orleans	42
	Seattle	37
Young	Indianapolis	18
	Atlanta	34
	Denver	24
	Columbus	19
	Memphis	27
	Nashville	21
	Dallas	22
	San Antonio	28
	Houston	21
	Jacksonville	23
	San Diego	16
	Phoenix	17

Source: Unpublished HUD estimates.

tralizing the old city's perverse fiscal endowments, the only politically feasible means to that end may be differential fiscal relief from the federal government. Paradoxically, then, the effects of such "discriminatory" formulas may be to create more equal fiscal environments.

But neutralizing the old city's fiscal legacy is only one step in an attack on the basic urban problem. That basic problem is viewed here not as one of city governments, but rather of city residents, and in particular of the minority poor. The next chapter considers the prospects for a more general urban strategy for dealing with the underlying urban problem—the continuing concentration of the minority poor in cities offering diminishing job opportunities.

9

THE CASE FOR DISPERSAL

Although the urban crisis as a crisis of social control has passed, an underlying structural problem remains. This enduring urban problem reflects the industrial obsolescence of the older metropolis, and above all of its declining central city. National shifts in population and production have stripped the industrial city of its traditional economic uses, while leaving its social use as a place in which the minority poor are effectively quarantined. The imbalance in the city's economic and social roles creates the prospect of a permanent urban underclass.

The laissez-faire policies the Nixon and Ford Administrations followed with respect to declining cities implicitly sanctioned their residual roles as reservations for the minority poor. As was suggested at the outset, a more positive federal role in the management of the old city's decline might be guided by either of two goals. A rejuvenation strategy would attempt to restore the old city's economic base, so as to provide the poor with marketable job skills.[1] By contrast, a dis-

1. We have left unexamined the complexities of ghetto labor markets. See in this regard Bennett Harrison, *Education, Training, and the Urban Ghetto* (Baltimore: Johns Hopkins Press, 1972). A more recent study, one that compares the human capital and dual labor market approaches to labor market processes influencing black employment changes, is Duane E. Leigh, *An Analysis of the Determinants of Occupational Upgrading* (New York: Academic Press, 1978).

persal strategy would aim for the gradual relocation of the minor-ity poor away from the industrial cities to areas offering superior job opportunities.

In the short run, of course, political considerations virtually all favor the redevelopment approach, if not complete inaction. For one thing, the nation's federalist system of political representation is struc-tured so as to pit individual states and localities in competition with each other for federal aid. Congressional legislation thus has a built-in bias favoring "place aid" to aid for individuals.

More subtly, a variety of attitudes and interests have created a cli-mate of public opinion that favors the channeling of jobs and other assistance to governments rather than to individuals—a practice that tends to tie the poor to declining cities. A recent survey, for example, found that 63% of the people polled favored a jobs-to-people ap-proach relative to the alternative, people to jobs (which was favored by only 20%). This preference was also the consensus view of the 500 or so participants of the January 1978 White House Conference on Bal-anced National Growth and Economic Development.[2]

Hence it is understandable that the Carter Administration's urban policy proposals contained elements of the redevelopment approach (and were symbolized by his pledge to rebuild the hopeless South Bronx), but no trace of the dispersal strategy.[3] The Carter plan might be described as a mixed strategy, involving as it does welfare reform, continued city fiscal relief, and temporary training measures like the city-administered CETA program.

Such an assuaging eclecticism has its merits, and it may be the best that can be had for now. But if this sort of short-run pragmatism becomes institutionalized as long-term strategy, the result seems easy to predict. A generation from now, the United States will still have a massive urban underclass, clustered in a network of ghettos stretching across the Manufacturing Belt. Such ghettos might surround dazzling downtown islands and gentrified inner neighborhoods. And the gen-try could well include a middle-class black contingent. Yet the minor-ity underclass would, in all probability, remain substantially intact.[4]

2. Both the survey results and the Balanced Growth conference are described in Neal R. Peirce, "Bringing Jobs to People," Dallas *Times Herald*, 26 February 1978.

3. A summary of the Carter proposals is *A New Partnership to Conserve America's Communities: A Status Report on the President's Urban Policy* (Washington: U.S. Government Printing Office, 1978).

4. William Julius Wilson, *The Declining Significance of Race: Blacks and Changing American Institutions* (Chicago: University of Chicago Press, 1979).

THE NEGLECTED ALTERNATIVE

The message of this study is that dispersal is more likely to have a desirable long-range impact than rejuvenation. Our findings suggest that a rejuvenation strategy would run against the tides of profound economic change—tides amplified by reenforcing institutional variables. While federal policies have clearly encouraged the cumulative decentralization of people and production, it does not follow that government now has the capacity to restore the prior locational regime.[5] Evolutionary processes on the scale we have considered typically foreclose such possibilities even as they open new opportunities.

Lest this conclusion smack of determinism, we might note the conclusions of Janet Roebuck, a British urban historian. She contends that only when an era's dominant technological influences are given their due can a realistic role for planning and policy implementation be defined.

> Society cannot simply decide to change the form and character of cities to make them conform to rationally determined aims and orders of priorities. . . . Social agencies that tinker with the form and character of the city cannot, therefore produce much . . . for *the force behind such readjustment plans is pathetically small compared with the tremendous pressures exerted by the economy and technological capacity.* Profound changes in the character of the city can only come from the sources from which they have always come, changes in economy and technology.[6]

To recognize that irreversible changes in the economic environment have taken place is the first step toward *taking responsibility for policies that perpetuate a dependent underclass.* In the long run, rejuvenation[7] seems to offer little if any hope of restoring the upgrading process. Hence the outlook for the minority poor will improve only when their fate is cut loose from that of the declining cities. Of course, the reverse is also true. Perhaps the surest means of easing the transition for the industrial cities is to free them from the burden of the minority poor.

These are strong statements—perhaps overly so. Yet there is a fur-

5. On the impact of past federal policies, see Roger J. Vaughan, *The Urban Impacts of Federal Policies* (Santa Monica: The Rand Corporation, 1977).

6. Janet Roebuck, *The Shaping of Urban Society* (New York: Charles Scribner's Sons, 1974), p. 231. (Emphasis added.)

7. Redevelopment's uncertain chances of success are the unifying (although implicit) theme of a recent collection of impressive papers, *Central-City Economic Development,* ed. Benjamin Chinitz (Cambridge, Mass.: Abt Associates, 1979).

ther reason for pessimism as to rejuvenation's prospects. Energy crisis or no, the spatial decentralization of economic activity will almost certainly continue. Quite apart from signs of a newly decentralized system of rural industrialization, a variety of factors point to the likelihood of a more dispersed *administrative* system.[8] There is every indication, in other words, that the 1980s will witness the early stages of a new technological epoch, a kind of global technetronic regime.

Extrapolating only slightly, the prospect in view is one of a new round of breakthroughs in communications technology, innovations likely to deprive central office districts of much of their present rationale. Telecommunications media and computer systems are already being linked up in global information networks. While inertia will soften the impact this new communications regime is likely to have, the eventual result could well be an erosion of the old cities' administrative employment on a scale matching the industrial exodus they have experienced since 1945. (As an aside, it would also tend to undermine the relative position of the younger metropolis relative to smaller settlements.)

In sum, the key requirement is a package of measures to help the minority poor respond to such changes in the spatial distribution of economic opportunity. Any such package would necessarily include relocation grants to individuals, improved training programs, and a national job information service. Within the metropolis, the series of measures Anthony Downs has proposed would constitute a vital component.[9] Finally, an essential concomitant of these relocation, training, and open housing measures would be welfare reform that effectively equalized payment levels, as adjusted for cost of living differences, nationwide.

Until some such package is pursued, it seems unlikely that any real headway will be made in improving the position of the urban underclass.

---

8. On the former tendency, see Robert Averitt, "Implications of the Dual Economy for Community Economic Change," in *Nonmetropolitan Industrial Growth and Community Change,* ed. Gene F. Summers (Lexington, Massachusetts: D. C. Heath and Co., 1979).

9. *Opening Up the Suburbs: An Urban Strategy for America* (New Haven: Yale University Press, 1973).

NAME INDEX

SUBJECT INDEX